THE ZODIAC REVISITED
Volume 2
Analysis and Fact-Based Speculation

THE ZODIAC REVISITED
Volume 2

Analysis and Fact-Based Speculation

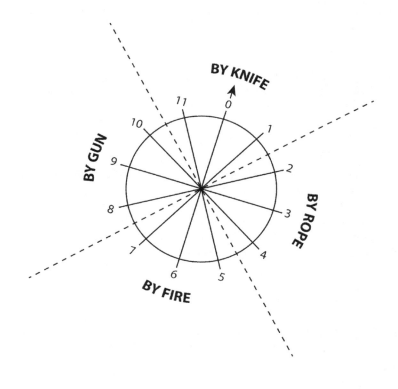

Michael F. Cole

Twin Prime Publishing
Folsom, California

ISBN 978-1-955816-00-7 (Hardcover Edition)
ISBN 978-0-9963943-1-4 (Paperback Edition)
ISBN 978-0-9963943-4-5 (ePub Edition)
ISBN 978-0-9963943-7-6 (Kindle Edition)

Library of Congress Control Number: 2020918394

Edited by Jennifer Huston
Cover design by Derek Murphy
Cover map © OpenStreetMap contributors

The front-page image of the September 30, 1969 edition of the *San Francisco Examiner* reproduced with permission.

Printed in the United States of America
First printing 2020

Published by Twin Prime Publishing
Folsom, California
zodiacrevisited.com

This book is dedicated to the memories of the following young men and women. Some definitely were victims of the man who called himself the Zodiac; others probably were. Regardless, all left this world much too soon and under circumstances of senseless tragedy.

- Robert Domingos
- Linda Edwards
- Johnny Ray Swindle
- Joyce Swindle
- Cheri Jo Bates
- David Faraday
- Betty Lou Jensen
- Darlene Ferrin
- Cecelia Shepard
- Paul Stine
- Richard Radetich
- Donna Lass

Although the passage of time has rendered the opportunity for justice an impossibility, it's my sincere hope that one day the world will know the name of the person or persons responsible for your unjust fates.

Contents

1

A Context for Analysis

For me context is key — from that comes the understanding of everything.[1]

Kenneth Noland, American artist, 1924–2010

In *The Zodiac Revisited, Volume 1*, we established the essential facts and basic chronology of the Zodiac case. As such, we are now in a position to consider the evidence more thoroughly in the hopes of developing a substantive understanding of the killer and his crimes. What were his motivations? Why did he act in certain ways as opposed to others? Was there a method to his apparent madness? What was the meaning behind the cryptic parts of the killer's, at times prolific, correspondence? What can we learn from the four ciphers sent by the killer, especially the three that remain unsolved?

Before we delve into those and other questions, it's important to build the proper foundation for the discussion by explaining the direction from which I'm approaching the subject. We should also consider a few other aspects of the case including conventional wisdom and some commonly held beliefs.

1.1   Statement of Position

To facilitate the analysis in the remainder of *The Zodiac Revisited*, I enumerate several of my beliefs regarding unresolved aspects of the case. Having this knowledge will make it easier to understand the direction and basis for some of the arguments that follow. Moreover, since I am explicitly calling out my beliefs and acknowledging that other people may not agree with these beliefs, I am going to avoid constantly qualifying my statements. Instead, I will simply state my beliefs as fact with the implicit understanding that some of them are not established facts. Taking this approach will make the material not only easier to write but also easier to read.

- The Zodiac was a persona adopted by a serial killer. The persona existed from the time of David Faraday's and Betty Lou Jensen's murders, December 20, 1968, until the man killed off the persona via the *Exorcist* Letter in January 1974. For activity outside of these two dates, the killer was acting as himself, not as the Zodiac.

- The killer was responsible for multiple murders prior to the adoption of the Zodiac persona.

- The killer murdered Robert Domingos and Linda Edwards in Gaviota, California, on June 4, 1963. These murders were likely his first.

- The killer murdered Johnny Ray Swindle and Joyce Swindle on February 5, 1964, in San Diego, California.

- After murdering Cheri Jo Bates in Riverside, California, on October 30, 1966, the killer authored the letter titled "The Confession" as well as the three additional notes sent six months after the crime.

- The Zodiac was responsible for all of the crimes and letters that are normally attributed to him.

- The Zodiac abducted Kathleen Johns and her infant daughter near Modesto, California, on March 22, 1970.

- The Zodiac murdered San Francisco Police Officer Richard Radetich on June 19, 1970.

- The Zodiac kidnapped and murdered Donna Lass on September 6, 1970, in South Lake Tahoe, California.

- The man killed off the Zodiac persona in the *Exorcist* Letter from January 1974.

- In addition to writing the *Exorcist* Letter as the Zodiac, the killer also authored other 1974 missives including the Citizen Card and the Red Phantom Letter, but not as the persona of the Zodiac.

- The killer may or may not have written the SLA Postcard; I'm on the fence.

- The killer did not write the 1978 "I Am Back with You" Letter.

Finally, let me point out that unlike many who have researched this case, I do not claim to know the identity of the Zodiac. Furthermore, I do not believe he was any of the commonly identified suspects. The man was likely someone who managed to avoid suspicion. While I do hope and believe that, eventually, the world will know the murderer's name, the insight I hope to provide in the following chapters is mostly in terms of understanding the man's actions. At best, this additional level of understanding will help identify the fugitive indirectly.

1.2   Terminology

This section contains a small collection of phrases that I use in the remainder of this book. Some of these terms will be explained in greater detail in later sections.

annotated Zodiac symbol: The Zodiac symbol from the cutout section of the 1969 Phillips 66 map sent with the Button Letter of June 26, 1970. The killer annotated the numbers 0, 3, 6, and 9, and added the instruction "0 is to be set to [magnetic north]."

Figure 1.1: The annotated Zodiac symbol

X'ed Zodiac symbol: The large Zodiac symbol used as the signature on the last page of the Bus Bomb Letter. This symbol is referred to as the *X*'ed Zodiac symbol because the killer marked five *X*s at various positions along the symbol's circle, as shown in the following figure.

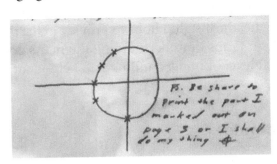

Figure 1.2: The *X*'ed Zodiac symbol

extended crimes of the Zodiac: This encompasses all the crimes that I believe the killer committed. These include the Southern California murders, the accepted Zodiac crimes, and the sometimes contested Zodiac crimes such as the murders of Officer Richard Radetich and Donna Lass.

extended victims of the Zodiac: All the victims associated with the extended crimes of the Zodiac

premeditated situational control: The killer's practice of planning for victim manipulation ahead of his attacks. This required constructing purposeful ruses and, to a lesser extent, selecting accommodating crime scene locations. See Section 2.2.

spatial information: The technique of communicating information through the relative placement of words, symbols, and figures. This concept is introduced in Section 3.3.1.1.

Lastly, I would like to point out that I sometimes refer to the killer as a psychopath and further assume that psychopathy — at least as it applies to this particular individual — is a form of mental illness. While most readers are unlikely to take issue with these two decisions, I acknowledge that, from an academic and professional perspective, one could argue against both of these points.

1.3   Conventional Wisdom

When a high-profile serial murderer goes unidentified for five decades, it's a safe bet that the subject will engender an abundance of opinion. With the Zodiac, the specific details of the case and its corresponding evidence have cultivated a diverse — or perhaps unconstrained and, at times, irresponsible — collection of public opinion. Yet, even within this loosely bounded set of beliefs, there are generally well-established common themes and fundamental core convictions that many people share. In the interest of using these ideas as analytical reference points, I review some of the commonly held beliefs in the following sections.

1.3.1 Social Torment

Many of the Zodiac's actions demonstrate a profound hatred toward women and, to a lesser extent, men who are able to forge meaningful relationships with women. By initially preying on couples seeking isolated locations, the killer clearly conveyed not only the type of victim — couples — against whom he was directing his murderous deeds but also the defining element of their existence that compelled him to the point of action, namely intimacy.

The commonly accepted, and almost certainly correct, interpretation of this element of victimology is that the killer suffered from a social deficiency that prevented him from forming normal, healthy relationships with members of the opposite sex. Likely, the man was ill at ease and awkward around women. As a result, he would have felt emotionally isolated from all people — from women because he undoubtedly blamed them for his failure and from men because he resented them for succeeding in areas where he, himself, could not.

A related point I will add here is that simply because the man was incapable of forming normal relationships with women does not mean that he necessarily had no relationships with women. It's certainly possible that he may have had one or more relationships. However, any such relationship likely would have been, in some way, abnormal. In other words, there would have been elements of the relationship that, if openly shared, would have struck most people as unusual or unhealthy.

A large subset of the extended Zodiac victims precisely reinforce this notion of social torment through their relevant symbolism — in other words, random couples attacked specifically at times when they were seeking romantic isolation. We see these circumstances with Robert Domingos and Linda Edwards (1963), Johnny Ray and Joyce Swindle (1964), David Faraday and Betty Lou Jensen (1968), Mike Mageau and Darlene Ferrin (1969), and Bryan Hartnell and Cecelia Shepard (1969). In fact, the symbolism was so strong that during the

Southern California time frame, after the murder of the Swindles, law enforcement recognized the probable motive and suggested that a "Sweetheart Slayer" was responsible.[2]*

A subset of the killer's other victims — Cheri Jo Bates, Kathleen Johns, and Donna Lass — serve to underscore that women were the primary source of the man's pathology. He preferred to kill couples in romantically isolated spots due to the powerful symbolism. But when other factors made the targeting of such couples impractical or otherwise inopportune, he would happily settle for victimizing lone women. He may have been jealous of men who could easily attract women and form normal, intimate relationships. But it was women whom he collectively blamed for rejecting him and, consequently, women for whom he reserved the vast majority of his hatred.

The murders of Paul Stine and Officer Radetich and the killer's obsession with threatening schoolchildren all serve to show that there were additional factors at work in the Zodiac's psyche, especially during the later part of his letter-writing campaign. Part of these deviations are likely the result of the killer compromising certain aspects of his criminal activity in the interest of expediency, for example, choosing to murder San Francisco cab driver Paul Stine after directing him to a preplanned destination. Other likely influences include issues related to the killer's use of methodology and an evolving motivation, especially in response to perceived slights from Martin Lee, San Francisco's chief of inspectors.

Nevertheless, the common thread that we find in all of the killer's actions is a disconnectedness with society. It appears to be this disconnectedness, in conjunction with some form of mental illness, that allowed the Zodiac to murder without remorse. And ultimately, it appears that this disconnectedness all stems from the killer's inability to form meaningful relationships with women.

---

*This accurate assessment likely motivated the killer to lay low for a while and change his victimology — in the form of attacking Cheri Jo Bates — once he did reemerge.

1.3.2 Attention-Craving Narcissism

Unlike most fugitives from justice, the crimes of the Zodiac only tell half of the story. The complementary, and arguably more interesting, half is embodied by the collection of correspondence penned at the hand of the killer himself. These letters provide a rare window into the psyche of an enigmatic murderer. And while many aspects of the writing raise more questions than they answer, there is no doubt that, on the whole, the communications provide a fascinating lens through which we can view the killer's motivations and thought processes.

One of the most prominent threads running throughout the series of communiqués is a clear and compelling need for attention. Starting with the very first letters from the Zodiac and the brilliantly orchestrated three-newspaper campaign surrounding the 408 cipher, the killer demonstrated a compelling psychological need to seek out attention and an impressive ability to get it through the manipulation of the media, law enforcement, and the public. As a result of the killer's additional crimes, further letter writing, and a willingness to transcend fundamental societal norms by threatening schoolchildren, the killer achieved the pinnacle of his infamy following the Stine murder. Nevertheless, he clearly continued to desire and receive attention until his initial fade from prominence and then later through his brief reemergence. Perhaps the most bizarre manifestation of the killer's need for attention was his extended effort to get the Bay Area public to wear Zodiac buttons. Though unsuccessful, the simple desire to have the people of the Bay Area acknowledge his existence in some publicly observable manner illustrates the extent to which the man wanted people to take notice and somehow embrace his persona.

Beyond the obvious craving for media attention, the killer repeatedly tried to convince readers of his communiqués that he was a clever individual. From the self-congratulatory description of attaching a penlight to his gun barrel, to taunting police by supposedly providing his name in the 408 cipher, to what he surely considered sophisticated bomb diagrams that evidenced his intellect; the man was obviously impressed with himself and he wanted to make sure that everybody else was too.

Finally, one specific dimension of this self-delight involved reveling in the sense of superiority that the killer derived from evading capture and outsmarting—as I'm sure he would describe it—law enforcement. We see evidence of this behavior in the Stine Letter, where he wrote that the "police could have caught me last night if they had searched the park properly..." Moreover, the Bus Bomb Letter is replete with examples of this trait, exemplified by the declaration: "The police shall never catch me, because I have been too clever for them." This attitude continued through the *Los Angeles Times* Letter, in which he asserted: "I am crack proof [*sic*]."

Even in the killer's final missive, the Red Phantom Letter, the presence of the man's self-absorption is lurking just below the surface in that he is projecting his own narcissism onto the target of his diatribe, Count Marco, whom he claims "... always needs to feel superior."

1.3.3 Intelligence

Conventional wisdom regarding the intelligence of the Zodiac is surprisingly unresolved. This question is one of those areas about which people find much to disagree. The most widely held belief appears to be that the killer possessed a moderately above-average IQ. However, detractors from this position have made arguments that span the spectrum of intelligence.

The lower end of the spectrum is perhaps best represented in the book *"This Is the Zodiac Speaking"* by Michael Kelleher and David Van Nuys. In that treatise, Kelleher suggests that the killer likely lacked formal education and held some type of menial job in his day-to-day life. Furthermore, Kelleher argues, the man likely possessed an unimpressive intelligence but possibly compensated for this lack of intelligence by applying himself as an "auditory learner" — a person who learns primarily through listening and experiencing knowledge in an auditory context.

At the other end of the spectrum, some people advocate that Ted Kaczynski was the Zodiac prior to his criminal career as the Unabomber. Ignoring for the moment his murderous deeds, one of Kaczynski's defining characteristics is a superior intelligence. He scored exceptionally high on an IQ test as a child and began attending Harvard at the age of sixteen. During graduate school, he accomplished some amazing intellectual feats en route to earning a PhD in mathematics from the University of Michigan. Obviously, those who argue that Kaczynski was the Zodiac necessarily believe that the killer was highly intelligent.

Generally, the Zodiac's use of ciphers indicates that he had an above-average cognitive ability, likely with an aptitude for mathematics and other similar types of analytical thought. Some have argued that with enough patience almost anyone could have learned to construct ciphers like those used by the Zodiac. While it's technically true that somebody with a different mental profile *could* have learned how to construct cryptograms as the Zodiac did, it's highly unlikely that such a person *would* have. The appeal of constructing ciphers and the meticulousness required to do it both point to a man whose thought patterns were more logical than artistic. Undoubtedly, the typical person who joins the American Cryptogram Association is substantially different than the average member of Americans for the Arts. It's safe to say that the killer likely had more in common with the former than the latter.

How the Zodiac's litany of spelling mistakes reflects on his intelligence depends on whether or not you take them at face value. Clearly, if they are a true and accurate indication of the man's ability to spell, then he almost certainly possessed below-average intelligence, or he may have been afflicted with a mental condition or learning disability that affected his spelling. If, on the other hand, the killer intentionally created the vast majority of the spelling mistakes simply as a way to mask his true cognitive ability, then the mistakes have little bearing on evaluating his intelligence; or perhaps, they are indicative of a manipulation scheme that, once again, points to an above-average intelligence.

Surprisingly, conventional wisdom provides little guidance in terms of evaluating the authenticity of the killer's spelling mistakes. Numerous people who are knowledgeable about the case disagree on the question, which is one of the reasons why the precise nature of the killer's intelligence remains unclear.

For his part, Martin Lee went on record as saying he felt " ... the bad grammar and misspelled words were employed purposely by the Zodiac for a reason not immediately understood."[3] I agree with this assessment, except that I would go further and add that the reason was likely to mask the true nature of the writer, both in terms of his ability to write and his underlying intelligence. Moreover, my interpretation of the evidence is that the killer possessed an intelligence that was well above average. I don't think he was on par with the likes of Kaczynski, but I do suspect that he received a post-secondary education and possibly even completed some graduate coursework.

1.3.4   Taking Credit

One particular theory that has, unfortunately, garnered widespread support in the last two decades or so is the idea that the killer had nothing to do with a number of the crimes for which he took credit. The basic idea is that instead of committing the crimes in question, the killer simply learned about them via newspapers or other similar means and then claimed responsibility for them. Supporters of this idea usually point to the crimes associated with Cheri Jo Bates, Kathleen Johns,* Richard Radetich, and Donna Lass as instances of this theory at work.

---

*In the case of Kathleen Johns, the suggestion is that she was not abducted by the Zodiac, she was mistaken in identifying her abductor as the Zodiac, and that once the killer learned of her story, he tried to take credit for the crime.

This "Taking Credit" theory received a significant and influential endorsement when James Vanderbilt wrote it into the screenplay of David Fincher's 2007 film *Zodiac*. In a moment of revelation, Paul Avery (portrayed by Robert Downey Jr.) explains to Robert Graysmith (played by Jake Gyllenhaal) how the Zodiac has taken credit for Kathleen Johns's abduction based on information that the killer gleaned from a *Modesto Bee* newspaper article.[4] This fictionalized scene is based on a longstanding and commonly held belief involving an actual *Modesto Bee* article that did, indeed, document Kathleen's ordeal.[5]

The specifics of this possible scenario, however, are flawed in that the *San Francisco Examiner* published an article with equivalent information on the same day.[6] It's unlikely that the killer would have sought out the obscure *Modesto Bee* article, especially when there would have been no need. Admittedly, this is more of a curious inconsistency than anything else. Nevertheless, the point is important for fully understanding the evolution of the Taking Credit theory. As for the validity of the theory itself, we'll explore all of the relevant crimes later in this book and in *Volume 3*. The analysis of these crimes will clarify why I consider the theory to be an analytical liability, not an asset.

But before leaving the subject, let me suggest that the scene from the movie is simply ironic. In reality, Paul Avery tracked down Kathleen Johns and told her story, at length, in an article for the *Chronicle*.[7] Moreover, after being motivated by a letter from a reader, Avery championed the idea the Bay Area killer known as the Zodiac had previously murdered Cheri Jo Bates in Riverside, California, going so far as to call the connection "definite."[8] Therefore, having a fictionalized Paul Avery endorsing a theory that is usually used to dismiss both of these victims just feels wrong.

1.3.5   Honesty

Conventional wisdom regarding the Zodiac is that he was dishonest — that he lied aggressively and often. The commonly held perception is that anything the man said should not be taken at face value. Many believe that he functioned as a psychopath who had no regard for telling the truth, and that he only chose to be honest when it furthered his own cause.

The primary basis for this belief is rooted in the fact that the Zodiac is known to have lied on numerous occasions: He lied when he claimed the solution to the 408 cipher would reveal his identity. He lied when he manipulated Bryan Hartnell and Cecelia Shepard through his ruse. And he lied by way of his ever-increasing murder score, which nobody believed.

Additionally, there are several instances where people often conclude the killer was lying based on related beliefs. For example, many suggest the killer lied in his description of the events immediately following Paul Stine's murder. People commonly believe that the cipher included in the "My Name Is" Letter does not, in fact, contain any form of the killer's name. And, of course, the people who subscribe to the Taking Credit theory believe all the claims related to those crimes are simply opportunistic lies.

Human nature also plays a role in terms of forming the conventional wisdom surrounding the Zodiac, both in general and with respect to his honesty in particular. We as human beings have a desire and a tendency to want our good guys to be wholly good and our bad guys to be wholly bad. We want our heroes to possess all the good qualities of a hero while having none of the bad qualities we associate with villains. Likewise, we want our villains to be plainly evil. When we start assigning evil traits to our heroes and noble attributes to our villains, the situation quickly becomes complicated and uncomfortable. As a rule, we'd prefer not to deal with such complexity.

So many decades after the fact, the persona of the Zodiac has evolved into a type of super-villain, and, hence, we naturally want to assign him all the undesirable traits we associate with evil. We want to label the man patently dishonest and move on.

Of course, reality cares little about how it comports with the expectations of human nature, and the world is rarely so black and white.

My views on the honesty of the killer are at odds with many people who are familiar with the case. All else being equal, I believe the Zodiac *wanted* to be honest. As is evident from his letters, he often exhibited a need to feel superior to law enforcement. Being honest was, in and of itself, a mechanism by which the killer could exert power over the police. In some sense, it was yet another taunting device. The killer would freely tell law enforcement the honest truth, and they were still powerless to stop him. To be sure, when circumstances required dishonesty, the man had no qualms about being dishonest. But for many of the subjects that cause others to speculate that the killer was lying, I suspect he was actually being honest.

Notes

1. Kenneth Noland, "Context," 1988, Speech at the University of Hartford.

2. Arthur Berman, "Honeymooner Killings Called Maniac's Work," *Los Angeles Times*, February 8, 1964, 1.

3. Jane Eshleman Conant, "Zodiac Boasts He'll Kill Again," *San Francisco Examiner*, November 12, 1969, 1.

4. David Fincher, director, *Zodiac*, Paramount Pictures, 2007.

5. "Woman Says Zodiac Killer Captured Her," *The Modesto Bee*, March 23, 1970, A–1.

6. "Rode with Zodiac, Woman Claims," *San Francisco Examiner*, March 23, 1970, 4.

7. Paul Avery, "New Evidence in Zodiac Killings," *San Francisco Chronicle*, November 16, 1970, 1.

8. Paul Avery, "Zodiac Link Is Definite," *San Francisco Chronicle*, November 17, 1970, 2.

2

Observations

If I have ever made any valuable discoveries, it has been owing more to patient observation than to any other reason.

Sir Isaac Newton, 1642–1727

As a first step in understanding the Zodiac, we look across the case evidence and make some disparate observations. This approach may feel disjointed, but it's a necessary imperfection. By reviewing these subjects, we will provide ourselves with important tools that will serve us well in the later analysis of more complicated topics.

2.1 The Importance of a Name

W. C. Fields once said: "It ain't what they call you, it's what you answer to." This thought is especially apropos to the persona of the Zodiac. It's important to remember that the killer chose the name "the Zodiac" himself. In fact, by the time the man first wrote the words "the Zodiac" in a letter, the press had already started referring to him as the "Cipher Killer."[1] Through the early stages of the reporting, no one referred to the man as the Zodiac and the name Cipher Killer gained considerable momentum, as evidenced by the fugitive's first front-page headline: "Police Dare Cipher Killer."[2] If the man would have been happy with the name Cipher Killer, he could have left it at that. Instead, he never once acknowledged the moniker Cipher Killer and continuously referred to himself as the Zodiac. Clearly, the name that he had chosen for himself had a special significance to him and he was determined to make sure that the media, law enforcement, the public, and everybody else used it. For these reasons, we should carefully consider the killer's name.

A detail that's often lost in the various tellings of the Zodiac story is that the persona's name includes the definite article — it is decidedly **the** Zodiac and not just Zodiac. At no point did the killer write: "This is Zodiac speaking;" it was always "This is the Zodiac speaking."*

Unfortunately, the most popular works on the subject of the killer — Robert Graysmith's book and David Fincher's movie (the latter having been based on the former) — are not only named *Zodiac*, but they both also continually refer to the killer as Zodiac.[3,4]

In *"This Is the Zodiac Speaking"*, the book that he coauthored, David Van Nuys correctly recognized the subtlety of the name and argued that the killer must have derived considerable satisfaction from describing himself as *the* Zodiac, as if he was emphasizing that there was one and only one Zodiac.[5] While I agree with this conclusion, I also believe that the killer's use of the definite article had more to do with how he chose the name and less to do with the additional satisfaction he may have felt because of it. More specifically, by the time the killer relocated from Southern California to the San Francisco Bay Area, sometime between the spring of 1967 and the fall of 1968,

---

*To be exact, there are two instances of the killer referring to himself simply as Zodiac (not the Zodiac): the return address on the Peek Through the Pines Card that apparently referenced Donna Lass's disappearance and the pasted-up Crackproof Card. Nevertheless, the killer clearly considered his name to be the Zodiac.

the experienced serial murderer committed to orchestrating a campaign of terror by way of a named, but otherwise anonymous, public persona. The man labored over the creation of the persona's different layers. Ultimately, he settled on the name "the Zodiac" based on the celestial concept that is always referred to precisely as *the* zodiac. Moreover, the name was interwoven into several aspects of the persona's existence, most notably the killer's methodology for murder as described in Chapter 3. This is why the man was insistent that he be called the Zodiac and never once considered the possibility of settling for being known as the Cipher Killer. The name was important to the man because the name had meaning, and the killer valued the meaning.

2.2   Premeditated Situational Control

In a number of the extended crimes of the Zodiac, the perpetrator employed what I've termed premeditated situational control, which is to say he spent considerable time and effort prior to the crime crafting an environment and a means by which he could effectively manipulate his victims. This process often involved choosing an accommodating crime scene, crafting a ruse, and fabricating dialogue designed to elicit specific responses from the people with whom he was interacting. In particular, the man's goal was to allay any fears or apprehensions his victims might have to the point that they would voluntarily put themselves in a vulnerable position. By the time these victims realized that things were not as they seemed, it was usually too late.

Of course, the killer only employed premeditated situational control when his method of attack necessitated some degree of cooperation from his victims. In a number of the killer's crimes, the man required no such cooperation and, hence, premeditated situational control did not play a role. The blitz-style attacks of David Faraday and Betty Lou Jensen on Lake Herman Road, Darlene Ferrin and Mike Mageau at Blue Rock Springs, and Richard Radetich fall into this category, as does the sniper-type assault on the Swindle newlyweds.

2.2.1   Cheri Jo Bates

In the case of Cheri Jo Bates, we are at a distinct disadvantage in terms of understanding the exact nature of the situational control simply because we are forced to rely upon the physical evidence at the crime scene and the anecdotal evidence provided by the killer himself. While much can be gleaned from those two sources, we are ultimately left with a sense of incompleteness regarding the details of the killer's interactions with Cheri.

Nevertheless, the type of situational control employed in the case of Cheri Jo Bates's murder can best be described as sabotage followed by a Good Samaritan ruse. By disconnecting the middle wire of the distributor on Bates's car, the killer was able to effectively construct a scenario under which he could inject himself into the situation, gain Cheri's trust, and manipulate her into voluntarily accompanying him to the area where, sometime later, she would lose her life.

A lone female struggling with automotive problems is one of the few scenarios under which a woman would likely accept the help of a male stranger with limited apprehension. Furthermore, this situation is especially well-designed in that the killer could spend time gaining the trust of his victim by pretending to work at fixing the problem, all the while knowing his actions would be in vain. The presence of greasy fingerprints and palm prints on the inside of the car clearly show that the killer did just that.

2.2.2   Bryan Hartnell and Cecelia Shepard

In contrast to the case of Cheri, the Zodiac left Lake Berryessa under the belief that both Bryan Hartnell and Cecelia Shepard had been fatally wounded. Because Bryan went on to recover from his wounds and Cecelia was able to communicate prior to the arrival of the ambulance, we have a very detailed account of the Zodiac's interactions with his victims. This account provides much insight into the killer's use of premeditated situational control.

Below are excerpts of the dialogue used by the Zodiac as recounted by Bryan Hartnell from his hospital bed the day after the attack.[6]

Cecelia: *What do you want?*

The Zodiac: *Now take it easy. All I want's your money. There is nothing to worry about. All I want is your money.*

Because the Zodiac was brandishing a firearm and donning an outfit that was certain to instill a sense of fear, it's not surprising to see that he initiates his conversation in a way that attempts to reassure his victims that "there is nothing to worry about." This initial dialogue is intended to set a tone that is diametrically opposed to the imagery that Bryan and Cecelia are confronting. More specifically, if there is a point during the encounter when Bryan or Cecelia are likely to attempt to physically confront or flee their assailant, it's within the first few moments. The Zodiac has fully considered his victims' thought processes and crafted his initial lines of dialogue based on these considerations.

Bryan: *[OK], whatever you say. I want you to know that I will cooperate so you don't have to worry. Whatever you say we'll do. Do you want us to come up with our hands up or down?*

The Zodiac: *Just don't make any fast moves. Come up slowly.*

Bryan: *But we don't have any money. All I have is 75 cents.*

The Zodiac: *That doesn't matter. Every little bit helps. I'm on my way to Mexico.*

The clear implication here is that the assailant is just passing through. He is trying to convey to Bryan and Cecelia that if they just do what he asks, he will soon be long gone. In other words, the urgency of the immediate situation — a stranger pointing a firearm at them — will soon give way to a scenario in which the assailant is hundreds of miles away, ultimately destined for another country, leaving Bryan and Cecelia to return to life as normal.

The Zodiac: *I escaped from Deer Lodge Prison in Deer Lodge, Montana.*

At first, this line of dialogue seems a bit curious if not downright odd. After further consideration, however, there is little doubt this fabrication is the product of a specific intention that likely required considerable forethought on the part of the Zodiac. There are at least two purposes served by this reference.

First, accomplished liars have an innate knack for embellishing their fabrications with subtle details that bolster their credibility. The Zodiac could have just said: "I escaped from prison." However, such a general statement is more likely to be dismissed out of hand. Instead, by mentioning a specific prison — and one that does indeed exist — along with a specific detail regarding the prison (its location in Deer Lodge, Montana), the Zodiac inherently sounds credible.

Second, the killer's specific choice of prison also is likely far from arbitrary. If he had chosen a prison that was well known and in relatively close proximity to the crime scene, it's much more likely that Bryan or Cecelia would have questioned why they hadn't heard about the escape on the news. But a prison break from some obscure, faraway prison would not raise any red flags. Moreover, if by chance either Bryan or Cecelia actually had been aware of Deer Lodge Prison, such knowledge would only serve to reinforce the apparent veracity of the assailant's claim.

The Zodiac: *I need some money to get there.*

Here again the Zodiac is attempting to establish the appearance of a clear cause-and-effect relationship. He is saying: "I have a need. If you satisfy this need, I will leave." This misdirection is intended to convince Bryan and Cecelia that the Zodiac's behavior is solely motivated by practicality. Of course, the killer's true motivations have no basis in practicality, which is why he must use such calculated lies.

Bryan:	*Well, is there any other thing you need?*
The Zodiac:	*Yes, one more thing. I want your car keys. My car is hot.*

In all likelihood, the killer planned on asking for the car keys from the beginning of the encounter. However, when Bryan disclosed that he only had seventy-five cents, it became more essential in terms of generating the intended perception. The Zodiac was on the verge of tying up Bryan and Cecelia. If the sum total of their loss amounted to seventy-five cents, the act of tying them up may have seemed disproportionate, which, in turn, might have led them to question the Zodiac's intentions. Under such conditions they may have feared that the perpetrator intended to do irrational harm, such as sexually assaulting Cecelia. By clearly communicating that he intended to take Bryan's car, the Zodiac established a significant monetary loss against which the act of tying up the young couple seemed to fit reasonably well into the rest of the killer's deception.

Bryan:	*I guess in all the excitement I don't remember where I put them. Let's see, are they in my shirt? In the ignition? On the blanket? Say, would you answer a question for me? I've always wondered. On T.V., movies and in an article in the Reader's Digest they say that thieves rarely keep their guns loaded. Is yours?*
The Zodiac:	*Yes, it is. I killed a couple of men before.*
Bryan:	*What? I didn't hear you.*
The Zodiac:	*I killed a couple of guards getting out of prison. And I'm not afraid to kill again.*
Cecelia:	*Bryan! Do what he says!*

The response from Cecelia is precisely the response the killer was attempting to elicit through his anecdote of killing prison guards. Again, this part of the conversation was likely fabricated ahead of time, although the man may not have planned an exact scenario under which he would bring up the claim of having killed previously. The key takeaway from the killer's dialogue to this point is that he's creating two starkly different aspects of his supposed reality. On the one hand, the message is: if you cooperate, everything will be over soon and you will be fine. On the other hand, if you choose not to cooperate, I am willing and able to kill you. Though vastly different in approach, these lines of conversation are actually aimed at achieving the same end, namely cooperation.

There is some more dialogue at this point, but little of it sheds additional light on the killer's use of premeditated situational control.

One last point to make in the Lake Berryessa case is that, obviously, the killer's use of an automatic weapon played an undeniable role in establishing and maintaining the situational control. The ruse was largely effective in terms of eliciting cooperation. But when Bryan protested being tied up, the killer ultimately had to point his weapon at Bryan's head before he was able to regain control. So, even though the killer had a strong desire not to use the gun — his goal was to murder his victims with a knife — the firearm was nonetheless instrumental in forcing events to play out as they did.

2.2.3   Paul Stine

The murder of Paul Stine involves what is perhaps the least interesting example of premeditated situational control. Paul was manipulated into following the directions of the killer simply because, as a taxicab driver, it was his job. The fugitive may have invested considerable forethought into deciding to use a cab and the details of the plan, including the location, which served him exceptionally well. But once the plans were solidified, the transaction involving Stine was unsurprisingly simple. Even the final instruction, to drive forward one more block, was reasonable. Nobody may fully understand exactly why he did it, but almost certainly, Paul would have done it without much of a second thought.

2.2.4   Kathleen Johns

Apart from Bryan Hartnell, Kathleen Johns and her daughter were the only other victims who survived an encounter with the Zodiac during which the killer employed some form of premeditated situational control. As with the crime at Lake Berryessa, the ability of Kathleen to recount considerable details of her interactions with the abductor provides us with valuable insight.

The situational control tactic employed by the Zodiac while abducting Kathleen Johns is exactly the same as that employed by the murderer of Cheri Jo Bates, namely sabotage followed by a Good Samaritan ruse. The primary difference between the two crimes is that Cheri's killer sabotaged her vehicle while it was unattended and, hence, she could more easily believe that the Good Samaritan had nothing to do with her automotive troubles. On the other hand, the Zodiac had to convince Kathleen Johns to pull over to the side of the road and then sabotage her car while she was acutely aware of his presence.

2.2.5   Robert Domingos and Linda Edwards

In terms of understanding the killer's use of premeditated situational control, perhaps the most valuable of the extended Zodiac crimes is not one in which he maintained control, but rather the one where he clearly lost it.

The murder of Robert and Linda is the earliest of all the crimes reasonably attributed to the man who would later be known as the Zodiac. Unlike most of the later crimes, this one was replete with mistakes. There was the failed attempt to burn down the shack in which the bodies were dumped and the surprising lapse in attention that resulted in the perpetrator leaving multiple boxes of ammunition at the site. But the single most problematic development happened during the commission of the crime when Robert apparently freed himself from the restraints and briefly struggled with the assailant prior to he and Linda unsuccessfully making a run for it.

Of course, Robert and Linda did not survive the attack. Nor did the killer ever write about the details of the Gaviota murders. More precisely, since these homicides happened at a time before the killer had evolved to the point of communicating with law enforcement and the public, we have no version of events other than what detectives could infer. In short, we know neither what was said nor any of the specifics about possible manipulation schemes that the perpetrator may have employed.

We do know, however, that the killer learned from his mistakes. In seven months' time, the man would move on to his next murderous outing, and, from that point forward, he would never again make the egregious errors that he had in Gaviota. Six years later, he would effectively re-create the Gaviota attack on an isolated shore of Lake Berryessa; except this time around, he maintained control from start to finish, likely modifying some aspects of his behavior based on the prior crime.

In fact, we can say that during the Gaviota attack, the killer either did not employ any type of premeditated situational control, or he made an attempt at doing so, but it wasn't executed well enough to yield the desired result. Either way, the man must have come away from the crime scene in Gaviota with an understanding that any later crimes in which he needed to interact with his victims would require better planning. By the time of the killer's third attack (the second being the sniper-style assassinations of Joyce and Johnny Ray Swindle, which required no victim interaction) the premeditated situational control used against Cheri Jo Bates was well thought out, sophisticated, and highly effective.

All of these examples serve to illustrate that premeditated situational control was a key element of the killer's modus operandi when the circumstances required that he interact with and elicit cooperation from his victims. Moreover, this thread of commonality running through the above crimes creates a meaningful connection.

This is especially important for the attacks on Cheri Jo Bates and Kathleen Johns. Though it's often overlooked or underappreciated, the same premeditated situational control tactic was used in both cases, namely automotive sabotage followed by a Good Samaritan ruse. This fact significantly increases the probability that the same man was responsible. And because the Zodiac is already suspected of the crimes — which were committed hundreds of miles apart — it's much more likely that the killer did, indeed, commit them rather than some other individual, as I will argue in Chapter 1 of *The Zodiac Revisited, Volume 3.*

2.3   Identity Establishing Behaviors

There are characteristics within the writings of the Zodiac that the killer seems to have consciously included in order to establish a pattern of behavior that further validates his identity. Though not nearly as effective as the bloodstained swatches of Paul Stine's shirt, these characteristics are worthy of attention, if for no other reason than because they provide insight into the thought processes of the killer.

2.3.1   Circles Instead of Dots

In many instances of the Zodiac's handwriting, both in letters and on envelopes, the killer used circles to dot the letter *i* and to create periods, colons, and semicolons. Sometimes, he filled in these circles, either partially or completely; other times, he did not. Although the killer did not consistently incorporate this distinguishing feature into all of his handwriting, the details regarding whether or not he used it suggest possibilities in terms of how we should interpret the trait.

Figure 2.1 shows the percentage of circles (either open, partially filled in, or completely filled in) used by the killer for most of the writing that he did as the persona of the Zodiac. Since the first three

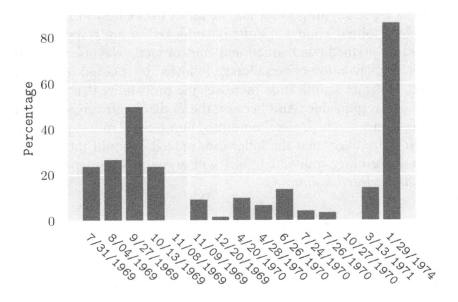

Figure 2.1: This bar chart shows how often the Zodiac used circles instead of dots in his public writings.

letters were all sent on July 31, 1969,* I've grouped them together and created a combined value. Admittedly, some of these percentages are based on a very small amount of text while others are derived from lengthier compositions. Despite these differences, it's still instructive to consider the trait in this way.

The data in the bar graph can be subdivided into three distinct sections. The first section consists of the killer's writing from the time he adopted the Zodiac persona, through the time he penned the Stine Letter. In this time period, his use of circles was relatively high, roughly around 30 percent. The next section consists of all of the killer's remaining communications except for the *Exorcist* Letter, which was written much later. The percentage of circles during this

_____

*To be precise, the letter received by the *Vallejo Times-Herald* on July 31, 1969, has been omitted because the quality is too poor. Additionally, the envelope from the August 4, 1969, letter is not available.

time frame dropped significantly — on average around 8 percent. Finally, the killer's use of the trait in the *Exorcist* Letter, his swan-song communiqué, is remarkably high at 86 percent.

What are we to conclude from this data? First, the trait is too inconsistent to be a component of the killer's normal handwriting. If he naturally used circles instead of dots, we would expect to see him using circles all the time. Rather, the circles are almost certainly the result of the man consciously altering the way that he writes. He's made a deliberate decision to change many of the dots into circles. But why?

The answer to the question is woven into the details surrounding the timing of the trait. The initial section of heavy usage corresponds to the time when the Zodiac was actively trying to convince the world that he was, indeed, the enigmatic Vallejo murderer. The letters of July 31, 1969, and August 4, 1969, each contain several enumerated details intended to prove that the author was who he claimed to be, namely the man responsible for the Lake Herman Road and Blue Rock Springs murders. Similarly, the killer wrote relatively little on Bryan Hartnell's car door at the Lake Berryessa crime scene, but most of what he wrote was intended to establish his identity, for example the location of his previous attacks ("Vallejo") and their dates.

Law enforcement's quibbling over whether the Zodiac was who he said he was eventually motivated the man to seek out and soon find a different mechanism for establishing his identity, which he did by sending swatches of Paul Stine's bloodstained shirt. Hence, starting with the Stine Letter, the killer had the means to prove that he was, in fact, the murderer of Paul Stine. Between October and December 1969, he used that method of proof on three separate occasions.

By the end of 1969 — even when letters from the Zodiac did not contain a swatch of Paul Stine's shirt — law enforcement had ceased squabbling over the killer's identity. At this point, nearly everyone involved in the investigation agreed that the fugitive was responsible for at least five murders. When a new letter arrived, it was usually authenticated by way of handwriting analysis and sometimes corroborated via the content, such as a mention of the bus bomb threat, which had been suppressed in the media. There was relatively little disagreement regarding the authenticity of probable Zodiac missives in this time frame — that didn't happen in any meaningful way until the Toschi debacle in 1978. (See Section 10.2 of *The Zodiac Revisited, Volume 1* for more information.)

Naturally, starting with the Stine Letter, the killer became less concerned with having to convince his readership that he was who he said he was. Doing so was either handled through the swatches of Paul Stine's shirt or simply not required. Similarly, the same time frame corresponds to the killer using circles instead of dots less frequently. Simply put, because the swatches of Paul Stine's shirt and the content of his communiqués proved he was the killer, he felt less of a need to modify his handwriting to verify his identity.

Last, but certainly not least, we have the *Exorcist* Letter. This is the final letter that the killer wrote as the persona of the Zodiac, and it was written nearly three years after the previous correspondence. It makes sense, then, that the killer would feel a need to reestablish his identity since he had been out of touch for so long. Interestingly, the killer could have more effectively reestablished his identity by sending another swatch of Paul Stine's shirt. However, he was either unable or otherwise unwilling to do so; his distinctive hand printing and other recognizable characteristics, including his use of circles instead of dots, would have to suffice.

Of course, the killer didn't just return to a previous level of using circles instead of dots. Instead, he amped up the usage to almost three times the level he had originally employed. This fact, again, reinforces the idea that the characteristic was a conscious behavior modification; in the *Exorcist* Letter he modified the behavior to an extreme. Furthermore, the excessive usage conveys an almost palpable desperation in terms of wanting to be recognized as the Zodiac.

2.3.2 Pasted-Up Patterns

Two of the pasted-up cards that the killer sent also exhibit some pattern-based similarities. The first such behavior is the use of hole punches in the preparation of the cards. On the Crackproof Card from October 5, 1970, the author cut out text from the *Chronicle* and pasted it onto a blank index card. He then punched thirteen holes in the card, one for each of the victims that he claimed to have murdered. With the Peek Through the Pines Card five and a half months later, the killer did something similar by attaching words and letters from different newspapers to a blank postcard. Again, he used a hole punch, this time to scallop the edges of the postcard and to make a single hole in the return address area that he used for the circular part of his signature Zodiac symbol.

The other peculiar characteristics common to these two pasted-up cards was the use of inverted text. On the Crackproof Card, the author inverted the entire postscript. For the Peek Through the Pines Card, he attached the single phrase "around in the snow" in an upside-down orientation. In both cases, the inverted text was placed in the lower-left corner of the card, however, the latter card did have additional text below it.

2.4 Avoidance of Weapon Reuse

One behavior that may seem surprising, especially on first consideration, is the killer's apparent unwillingness to reuse any of his weapons. The man clearly had a strong desire to establish himself as the perpetrator of most of the Zodiac crimes. If he had used the same weapon for even a subset of the murders that involved firearms, law enforcement easily could have connected the crimes together through ballistics. Very quickly, there would have been little doubt that the same person was responsible.

Police initially believed the same 9 mm weapon had been used in the Blue Rock Springs attack and the murder of Paul Stine. This was a logical bit of speculation given that the Zodiac took credit for both crimes and both involved a 9 mm handgun, a caliber that was relatively rare at the time. Not until ballistics analysis came back negative did the police realize that the killer had actually used two different 9 mm weapons.[7]

Interestingly, investigators had suspected that a single man was responsible for the 1963 sweetheart slayings in Gaviota and the 1964 newlywed murders in San Diego. In both cases, the killer had used a .22-caliber weapon which had led police to be hopeful that the ballistics would match. However, they did not.[8]

Similarly, when investigators compared the ballistics of the .22-caliber weapons that the killer used to carry out the Lake Herman Road murders and the 1963 Gaviota murders, the guns did not match. It was yet another promising possibility that ultimately led nowhere.

With other facts suggesting that the same man committed all these murders, I interpret law enforcement's inability to match any of the weapons as a likely indication that the killer consciously chose to vary his weapon, likely from the very beginning in 1963.

The advantage of this behavior — from the killer's perspective — is the uncertainty that it creates. Had the Zodiac used the same weapon for many of his crimes, it would have allowed law enforcement to connect those crimes easily. However, under this scenario everyone involved would have had a more difficult time believing that the Zodiac was responsible for crimes involving weapons that had *not* been connected to the killer. This situation would have diminished the killer's ability to terrorize the people of the Bay Area.

Likely, in the early 1960s, prior to adopting the persona of the Zodiac, the killer chose to vary his murder weapon simply as a matter of practicality to reduce the probability of getting caught. Since he was targeting strangers, changing his geographic location, and varying his choice of weapon, the killer was providing police with very little that they could use to connect his crimes. Prior to the murders of Joyce and Johnny Ray Swindle in San Diego in 1964, Santa Barbara County Sheriff James Webster warned law enforcement agencies in the surrounding Southern California coastal areas that the killer he was pursuing may well strike again in a different but relatively nearby location.[8] So when Joyce and Johnny Ray were gunned down, Sheriff Webster was quick to suggest that it was likely the work of the same killer. However, when ballistics showed that different weapons were used in the two cases, investigators were unable to prove the connection.

By the time the killer moved on to the Bay Area, his motivations had likely changed. No longer was he primarily concerned with frustrating law enforcement's efforts to connect his crimes. In fact, he *wanted* police to connect the crimes that he'd committed, at least initially. But longer term, he likely derived significant satisfaction from the uncertainty of the situation he had set into motion. For much of the Zodiac era, anytime there was a murder or an attack that resembled the work of the fugitive, even in the slightest, people from all parts of the Bay Area were quick to suggest that the Zodiac might be responsible. For example, from 1969 to 1971, the *Chronicle* ran no less than nine stories suggesting the possible involvement of the Zodiac in crimes that later proved to be unrelated to the criminal.[9-17] During this time frame, the uncertainty of the killer's actions — partially created by his practice of using different weapons — escalated his status to a sort of bogeyman, which he used to terrorize the people of the Bay Area to great effect.

Clearly, this type of uncertainty was consistent with the change that the Zodiac announced in the Bus Bomb Letter, where he claimed that he would no longer take credit for his crimes. The change came about, ostensibly, as a result of Chief of Inspectors Martin Lee's unflattering characterizations of the murderer. Importantly, by the time the Zodiac made that announcement, he had already committed all the murders that police can definitely attribute to him. The fact that the killer had been changing his weapon of choice from the very beginning suggests that this uncertainty and the type of fearful ambiguity that goes with it may have been his goal all along.

2.5 Female Victim Focus

One observation that several people have made over the years is that the Zodiac appears to have concentrated on killing his female victims. This conclusion is based on the first three attacks of the Zodiac. In each case, the killer assaulted a couple seeking romantic isolation. In all three instances, the female victim did not survive. Yet, in two of the three attacks, the male victim, though gravely wounded, did survive.

Many people use this observation to suggest that the killer's lethal motivations were more acutely focused on the female — in other words, that the woman was the primary target of his psychopathology. While I don't disagree with the conclusion, I do disagree with reaching it on the basis of the two male victims surviving. In both cases, there were additional contributing factors that influenced who lived and who died.

A related behavior that's relevant is that the Zodiac always sought to eliminate the male threat first. He viewed the male half of the couple as dangerous and understood that if he was going to lose control of the situation, it would likely be due to an altercation with the man. Therefore, he shot David Faraday before Betty Lou Jensen; he shot Michael Mageau before Darlene Ferrin; he had Cecelia Shepard tie up Bryan Hartnell first, and then he stabbed Bryan before Cecelia.

In the case of Blue Rock Springs, the killer's desire to eliminate the male threat meant that he approached Darlene's vehicle from the passenger's side, where Mageau was seated. Therefore, Darlene was positioned behind Mageau with respect to the shooter. Consequently, Darlene was struck by bullets that were originally fired at Mageau. In contrast, none of the shots intended for Darlene struck Mageau. Additionally, Mageau (as the killer described in his letter) struggled strenuously to get out of the line of fire and disrupt the shooter's aim, whereas Darlene was unable to interfere with the assailant's shooting. Taken together, these circumstances translated into Darlene being fatally wounded whereas Mageau was not.

At Lake Berryessa, interestingly, the opposite dynamic played a role in the final outcome. Bryan immediately committed to a tactic of feigning death — mostly because he was unable to do much else — which resulted in the killer stabbing him only six times. Cecelia, on the other hand, put up an intense struggle against her assailant, which ultimately ensured that she was more gravely injured. The extent of her injuries coupled with the remoteness of the crime scene were the primary reasons she didn't survive.

2.6 Timing and Logistics

One potentially revealing aspect of the Zodiac's behavior is that during his time in San Francisco, he restricted his murderous activity to weekends. The Lake Herman Road crime happened on a Friday night. The next three attacks — Blue Rock Springs, Lake Berryessa, and Presidio Heights — all took place on Saturdays. Kathleen Johns's abduction occurred late on a Sunday evening. Donna Lass's disappearance in South Lake Tahoe, the possible Zodiac crime farthest away from San Francisco, happened around 2 a.m. on the Sunday of Labor Day weekend in 1970. San Francisco Police Officer Richard Radetich *was* likely a victim of the Zodiac, although his murder occurred during the predawn hours of a Friday morning, which technically violates the weekend behavioral pattern, albeit minimally.

The obvious implication of this apparent pattern is that the killer held a conventional nine-to-five job that prevented him from acting during standard working hours. Moreover, the circumstances of his employment, or possibly other aspects of his life, seemed to make him uncomfortable acting during weekday evenings. In the words of criminal profiler Sharon Pagaling Hagan: "He was a weekend offender, and that shows us that he was employed Monday through Friday. And he was very busy during those days. He was not free to commit crimes. He was not free to hunt for victims."[18]

Beyond the crimes themselves, the killer sent a number of his communiqués using public mailboxes within San Francisco, often on weekdays. This fact suggests that he may have been in or very near the city as part of his daily routine. Specifically, the man may have sent the letters on the way to or from work, or possibly during his lunch break.

Two of the three Southern California crimes violate this pattern of weekend activity. The 1963 Gaviota murders were committed on a Tuesday afternoon. Eight months later, the Swindles were gunned down in San Diego on a Wednesday evening. Two and a half years after that, Cheri Jo Bates was murdered on a Sunday night. Interestingly, however, her killer mailed The Confession letters from Riverside such that they were postmarked on Tuesday afternoon. If the man lived in Southern California at the time, but not close enough to Riverside that he could conveniently mail the communiqués — as I believe he did — then he would have had to explicitly make a trip to Riverside. This scenario also hints at Tuesday being a day during which the killer had some free time.

These facts, in conjunction with the Zodiac's very structured San Francisco behavior, make the case that the killer did not have a job with conventional working hours during his time in Southern California. However, it's difficult to read too much into this conclusion. He may have been a student, he may have been employed in a job that involved unconventional shift work, or he simply may have been unemployed; although this latter possibility just feels unlikely. Regardless, subsequent events suggest that sometime in 1967 or 1968, he moved to the Bay Area and found work at a nine-to-five job.

Notes

1.　"Vallejo Mass Murder Threat Fails," *San Francisco Sunday Examiner & Chronicle*, August 3, 1969, A9.

2.　"Car Door Message Revealed," *San Francisco Examiner*, September 30, 1969, 1.

3.　Robert Graysmith, *Zodiac*, New York: Berkley Books, 1987.

4.　David Fincher, director, *Zodiac*, Paramount Pictures, 2007.

5.　Kelleher, Michael D. and Van Nuys, David, *"This Is the Zodiac Speaking"*: *Into the Mind of a Serial Killer*, Westport, Conneticut: Praeger, 2002, p. 54.

6.　John Robertson, "Supplementary Crime Report: Case No. 105907," September 28, 1969, Accessed November 25, 2020, *http://zodiacrevisited.com/book/ncsd-1969-09-28-p26*.

7.　Paul Avery, "The Search for Zodiac's 4 Weapons," *San Francisco Chronicle*, October 22, 1969, 1.

8.　Arthur Berman, "Honeymooner Killings Called Maniac's Work," *Los Angeles Times*, February 8, 1964, 1.

9.　"Savage Killing of A Baby Girl," *San Francisco Chronicle*, October 20, 1969, 1.

10.　"Arsenic in Soft Drink — Zodiac?" *San Francisco Chronicle*, November 8, 1969, 3.

11.　"I've Killed Seven, The Zodiac Claims," *San Francisco Chronicle*, November 12, 1969, 1.

12.　Paul Avery, "Berserk S.F. Man Is Slain," *San Francisco Chronicle*, November 22, 1969, 3.

13.　Paul Avery, "A Zodiac-Like Ambush," *San Francisco Chronicle*, November 26, 1969, 1.

14.　"New Cabbie Attack — Hint of Zodiac," *San Francisco Chronicle*, January 26, 1970, 1.

15.　"Bizarre 'Zodiac' Murder," *San Francisco Chronicle*, April 20, 1970, 1.

16.　"Clues Found on Search for Coed," *San Francisco Chronicle*, March 1, 1971, 2.

17.　Paul Avery, "Knife Murder of Girl — Fears of Zodiac," *San Francisco Chronicle*, April 13, 1971, 1.

18.　David Prior, director, *This Is the Zodiac Speaking*, Paramount Home Entertainment, 2008.

3

A Methodology for Murder

Though this be madness, yet there is method in't.

Polonius, from William Shakespeare's *Hamlet*

Now that we've created a context for our analysis and made some broad observations regarding the totality of the evidence, we're in a position to analyze a complex aspect of the Zodiac's behavior, namely his use of a methodology to dictate many of his actions. As we will see, the existence of this methodology is a logical conclusion based on straightforward interpretations of fundamental clues.

A killer employing a methodology such as the one described herein is rare, if not unique, in the annals of serial murder. Certainly, this behavior offers us some insight into the psychology of the killer. Not only does it require a high degree of premeditation, discipline, and structure, but it hints at a cerebral person capable of abstract thought. More than that, however, the methodology also helps explain one of the key questions raised by the case: how did the fugitive manage to evade capture? To be sure, he had more than his fair share of luck. However, luck in and of itself would not have been enough for the killer to get away with his crimes. Beyond luck, he benefited from the unpredictable and confusing ways in which he committed his crimes, which ultimately stemmed from his adherence to a methodology.

3.1   A Point of Confusion

On Friday, October 17, 1969, the *Chronicle* published a story explaining that police were consulting an astrologer " ... to give detectives a background in the exotic science that apparently fascinates the killer."[1] The claim that the killer was fascinated by astrology was based upon nothing more than the Zodiac's name.

This story illustrates a problem that has plagued the Zodiac investigation since the August 4, 1969, letter to the *Examiner* in which the killer first used his self-assigned moniker. Modern pop culture has so conflated the concepts of the zodiac and astrology that most people believe the two are one and the same. In point of fact, the two concepts are separate and distinct but related. In particular, the zodiac is simply the division of the nighttime sky into a set of twelve constellations, each of which exists within a thirty-degree slice of the sky. The basis for the zodiac is observational science and astronomy. Astrology, on the other hand, is the belief that the positioning of the constellations embodied by the zodiac, especially at the time of a person's birth, influences, if not preordains, certain aspects of his or her behavior. The basis for these beliefs is superstition.

Given this relationship, it's important to understand that the concept of the zodiac *can* exist without astrology. The reverse, however, is not true; astrology *cannot* exist without the zodiac. As you will see, the evidence in the case of the Zodiac clearly indicates that the killer took his name from the observational-science aspect of the zodiac, not from astrology.

3.2   The Compass Rose

Figure 3.1 depicts the annotated Zodiac symbol, as drawn by the killer, on the cut-out section of a Phillips 66 map that he sent along with the Button Letter on June 26, 1970.

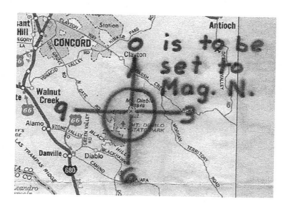

Figure 3.1: The compass rose inspired this annotated Zodiac symbol from the 1969 Phillips 66 map

In order to understand this annotated Zodiac symbol, one must first be familiar with the concept from which it was derived — namely, the compass rose. A compass rose is a figure used to orient direction on maps or charts. The one drawn by the Zodiac is a version of a standardized compass rose that appears on nautical charts, as shown in Figure 3.2.

As can be seen in this figure, the compass rose used in nautical charts consists of two separately aligned circles. The outer circle is aligned to true north. The inner circle is aligned to magnetic north.

Magnetic north is the northern direction as indicated by Earth's magnetic fields. In more familiar terms, it is the direction that a magnetic compass will point. Because Earth's magnetic fields are in a constant state of flux, the relationship between true north and magnetic north — an angle that is sometimes referred to as magnetic declination — changes over space and time. In other words, two different physical locations almost certainly will have two different magnetic

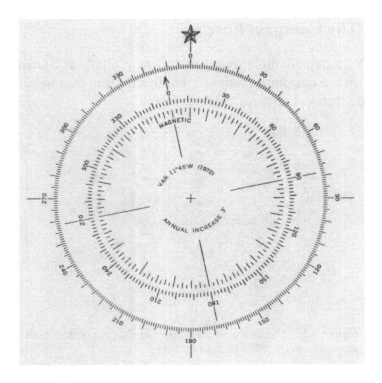

Figure 3.2: An example of a compass rose from a nautical chart

declinations, and a given magnetic declination for a single location will actually change with the passage of time.

The annotated Zodiac symbol and the standard compass rose used in nautical charts have the following in common:

- both appear on maps
- both are constructed from graduated circles
- both graduated circles are numbered from 0
- both give primary emphasis to the lines associated with the four cardinal directions

- both graduations emphasize the thirty-degree divisions — the compass rose explicitly and the annotated Zodiac symbol through its implied numbering

- both have an arrow on the line associated with 0

- both call out magnetic north; the annotated Zodiac symbol instructs "0 is to be set to Mag. N."; the standard compass rose includes an internal magnetic compass rose that has its 0 axis aligned with magnetic north.

These similarities are too numerous and too compelling to dismiss as mere coincidence. Clearly, the Zodiac was aware of the nautical-style compass rose, and, furthermore, he clearly fashioned his annotated Zodiac symbol on the Phillips 66 map after this type of compass rose.

3.2.1   Celestial Navigation

Given that the Zodiac, through his own actions, established this connection between his criminal persona and the subject of nautical navigation, the link clearly deserves further consideration. In particular, the connection raises the question: are there other aspects of nautical navigation that may have played a role in terms of influencing the killer's persona or his actions?

One of the most well-known references for the subject of nautical navigation is a book entitled *The American Practical Navigator*, originally by Nathaniel Bowditch. This compendium has been published and continuously updated since 1802 — first privately and later via the US government after the navy purchased the rights to the book in 1867.

In order to ascertain the potential for this book or its subject matter to have served as inspiration for the Zodiac, I obtained a copy of the 1966 edition, which the killer may have used.

The American Practical Navigator is divided into eight parts. One of these eight parts, some 225 pages, is dedicated to the subject of celestial navigation or navigation through the use of the nighttime sky.

Contained within this part of the book is a chapter entitled "Navigational Astronomy," which defines and describes the concept of the zodiac via the following two paragraphs [emphasis added]:

> *The zodiac is a circular band of the sky extending [eight degrees] on each side of the elliptic. The navigational planets and the moon are within these limits. **The zodiac is divided into [twelve] sections of [thirty degrees] each**, each section being given the name and symbol ("sign") of the constellation within it....*
>
> *The sun remains in each part for approximately one month. **When the names were assigned, more than 2,000 years ago, the sun entered Aries at the vernal equinox, Cancer at the summer solstice, Libra at the autumnal equinox, and Capricornus at the winter solstice.** Even though this is no longer true because of precession of the equinoxes, The American Ephemeris and Nautical Almanac still lists the sun as entering these constellations at the times of the equinoxes and solstices, for this has come to be their principal astronomical significance. **The [pseudoscience] of astrology assigns additional significance, not recognized by scientists, to the positions of the sun and planets among the signs of the zodiac.**[2]*

The definition of the zodiac is a bit technical, but the accompanying illustration from *The American Practical Navigator*, shown in Figure 3.3, provides clarity.

The above two paragraphs provide significant insight into the persona of the Zodiac. One major point is that the compass rose the killer himself drew — which was not immediately recognizable as relating to the concept of the zodiac — easily leads to a reference book in which the zodiac is defined. But not only is it defined, it's defined with the caveat that "the [pseudoscience] of astrology assigns additional significance, not recognized by scientists...."

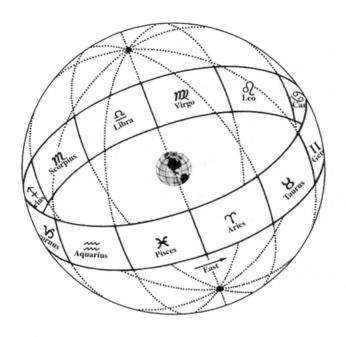

Figure 3.3: A pictorial representation of the zodiac from *The American Practical Navigator*

With nothing in the case evidence to suggest that astrology played a role in the persona of the Zodiac and the above evidence supporting that the killer took his self-assigned moniker from the general concept of the zodiac, as it pertains to celestial navigation, it's logical to conclude the latter. Furthermore, subsequent analysis will continue to support this position.

In fact, in this regard, the choice of the name "the Zodiac" is fascinating. Few words or phrases in the English language are so widely known in our pop culture and yet, simultaneously, so laden with alternate, esoteric meaning. In this sense, the killer may well have derived satisfaction in knowing that his moniker was misinterpreted by much of the general public.

In particular, the distinction between the underlying meaning of the term "the zodiac" and the popular astrological context of the phrase may have served to accentuate the generational gap present between the killer and his victims. The killer was likely thirty to forty years old during his reign of terror. In contrast, his victims were much younger, ranging in age from sixteen to twenty-two, with the exception of Paul Stine, who was twenty-nine at the time of his death. In the mid- to late-1960s, young people embraced astrology in ways that heightened its acceptance. As such, the killer may have chosen his self-assigned name to fundamentally differentiate himself from his victims. In pop culture and particularly with the youthful generation — or "kids" to use the killer's vernacular — the term "the zodiac" was generally only known in the pseudoscientific, astrological sense of the phrase, whereas the killer employed the moniker based on its true scientific meaning.

It's unlikely that the Zodiac chose his moniker because of this generational differentiation — there are just too many alternative ways in which the name is relevant for that to be true. However, this characteristic of the name may well have served as a secondary or tertiary reason why the killer felt the moniker was a good choice. Furthermore, as law enforcement and the media continually made reference to the astrological interpretation of the name, the killer likely felt an ongoing sense of satisfaction and even superiority, perhaps mixed with a tinge of frustration at the thought of not being understood.

3.2.2   The Zodiac Circle

Another key point we can glean from those two paragraphs in *The American Practical Navigator* is the importance of the killer's symbolic use of a circle divided into twelve equal slices, which most people are probably familiar with due to some knowledge of astrology. The above description, however, makes it clear that such a zodiac circle actually represents the underlying celestial concept. Moreover, the killer's various references to circles divided into twelve equal sections — in the form of the *X*'ed Zodiac symbol and the annotated Zodiac symbol, with the latter's implied numbering of 0 through 11 on the Phillips 66 map — are abstract, but straightforward, references to the concept of the zodiac.

In fact, from both the *X*'ed Zodiac symbol and the annotated Zodiac symbol, we can see that the killer's self-assigned symbol is actually a logical abbreviation of a full zodiac circle.

3.2.3 Solstices and Equinoxes

The third key takeaway from *The American Practical Navigator*'s description of the zodiac is the essential role that the solstices and equinoxes play in terms of the *definition* of the concept. The importance of this point cannot be overstated. **These four astronomically significant times of the year are fundamentally related to the origin of the zodiac; they are essential to what the zodiac *is* as a concept.** This is one of the most important observations we can make about the name the killer chose for his public persona. As will be evident later, part of the Zodiac's methodology included attempting to time his actions in accordance with the solstices and equinoxes. This relationship between the concept of the zodiac and these four times of the year is *why* he chose to do it.

To better understand the solstices and equinoxes, we can once again turn to *The American Practical Navigator*. On page 371, the author provides the following description [emphasis is original]:

> *On or about June 21, about ten or eleven days before reaching aphelion, the northern part of [Earth's] axis is tilted toward the sun. The north polar regions are having continuous sunlight; the northern hemisphere is having its **summer** with long, warm days and short nights; the southern hemisphere is having winter with short days and long, cold nights; and the south polar region is in continuous darkness. This is the **summer solstice**. Three*

*months later, about September 23, [Earth] has moved a quarter of the way around the sun, but its axis of rotation still points in about the same direction in space. The sun shines equally on both hemispheres, and days and nights are the same length over the entire world. The sun is setting at the north pole, and rising at the south pole. The northern hemisphere is having its **autumn**, and the southern hemisphere its spring. This is the **autumnal equinox**. In another three months, on or about December 22, the southern hemisphere is tilted toward the sun and conditions are the reverse of those six months earlier, the northern hemisphere having its **winter**, and the southern hemisphere its summer. This is the **winter solstice**. Three months later, when both hemispheres again receive equal amounts of sunshine, the northern hemisphere is having **spring** and the southern hemisphere autumn, the reverse of conditions six months before. This is the **vernal equinox**.*

The word "equinox," meaning "equal nights," is applied because it occurs at the time when days and nights are of approximately equal length all over the earth. The word "solstice," meaning "sun stands still," is applied because the sun stops its apparent northward or southward motion and momentarily "stands still" before it starts in the opposite direction.[3]

Again, the accompanying illustration, shown in Figure 3.4, helps to clarify a rather technical description.

Readers familiar with Robert Graysmith's book entitled *Zodiac* will recall that the author theorized the Zodiac was planning some of his activities around the solstices and equinoxes. Unfortunately, Graysmith was not able to make a compelling argument as to why the killer might have chosen to act during those times. Furthermore,

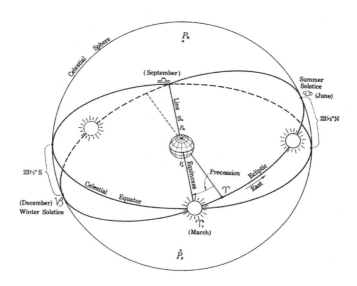

Figure 3.4: An illustration explaining the solstices and equinoxes from *Bowditch*

he confused the issue by attempting to incorporate holidays, astrology, horoscopes, and phases of the moon into his theory, all of which likely had nothing to do with influencing the killer's actions.[4]

Table 3.1 documents the relationship between various Zodiac events and their corresponding solstice or equinox. As you can see, there is compelling, albeit imperfect, correlation.

Given that we know the Zodiac was predisposed to act on weekends, we should consider any alignment that corresponds to an adjacent weekend, whether before or after, as perfect alignment. Using this criterion, six of the ten events align perfectly. Two celestial events are altogether unaccounted for and two others are associated with Zodiac activity via a correlation that is less than perfect.

Contrary to what the SFPD says, I believe Richard Radetich was a legitimate victim of the Zodiac. In addition to other evidence that supports this belief, his murder is perfectly aligned with the summer solstice of 1970.

Season	Event	Date	Zodiac Event	Date	Error
Winter	Solstice	12/21/1968	Lake Herman Rd.	12/20/1968	-1
Spring	Equinox	3/20/1969	No Known Event	N/A	N/A
Summer	Solstice	6/21/1969	Blue Rock Springs	7/ 4/1969	+13
Autumn	Equinox	9/23/1969	Lake Berryessa	9/27/1969	+4
Winter	Solstice	12/22/1969	Belli Letter	12/20/1969	-2
Spring	Equinox	3/21/1970	Kathleen Johns	3/22/1970	+1
Summer	Solstice	6/21/1970	Richard Radetich	6/19/1970	-2
Autumn	Equinox	9/23/1970	Donna Lass	9/ 6/1970	-17
Winter	Solstice	12/22/1970	No Known Event	N/A	N/A
Spring	Equinox	3/21/1971	Pines Card	3/22/1971	+1

Table 3.1: The relationship between the Zodiac's actions and the solstices and equinoxes

The first Zodiac event that demonstrates some degree of misalignment is the attack at Blue Rock Springs, which occurred nearly two weeks after the 1969 summer solstice. If we accept the assumption that the killer was, indeed, attempting to align his crimes with the solstices and equinoxes, then it's unclear why this one deviates from the pattern. However, we can speculate as to a couple of possible reasons.

First, it's useful to note that the Zodiac acted *after* the solstice. This may be an indication that the killer had some degree of trouble perpetrating his intended crime. We know from William Crow's story* that the Zodiac almost certainly had at least one failed attempt in committing the Lake Herman Road murders. We also know from Mike Mageau's description of events that the killer took some degree of precaution by first identifying his potential victims and then temporarily leaving, presumably to ensure that the coast was clear in at least one direction. In the case of Lake Berryessa, the Zodiac likely spent time observing the three young women who reported witness-

---

*Unbeknownst to them at the time, William Crow and his girlfriend almost certainly escaped from the Zodiac at the exact location where David Faraday and Betty Lou Jensen were gunned down just an hour and a half later. See Section 2.1 of *The Zodiac Revisited, Volume 1.*

ing a man behaving suspiciously. Even in the case of the Stine murder, we know the killer, at the last minute, instructed Stine to drive one block farther than the originally stated destination.

Given all of these indications of events unfolding in a less than perfect manner, it's not too much of a stretch to imagine an outing during which the killer failed to find acceptable victims under a set of circumstances that were sufficiently accommodating.

Another thought regarding the Blue Rock Springs attack is that the crime effectively represented a duplication of the Lake Herman Road murders. The victims were similar, the geographic location was essentially the same (differing by a distance of approximately four miles), and the type of weapon — a gun — was identical apart from the specifics of caliber. We know that the Zodiac would soon begin varying certain aspects of his crimes. Perhaps in the two weekends prior to July 4, 1969, the killer attempted to commit murders in which he varied some aspect of the methodology but failed. In the wake of this failure, he may have concluded he was running out of time and opted to re-create the type of crime that had worked for him previously.

It's curious to note that the Blue Rock Springs attack does align well with the celestial event known as aphelion, which occurs approximately ten days after the summer solstice and is also mentioned in *The American Practical Navigator*'s discussion of the solstices and equinoxes. While it's tempting to consider the idea that the killer may have somehow opted to align his attack with aphelion, it's the solstices and equinoxes that are a fundamental part of the zodiac not aphelion. Therefore, we simply have to accept that the timing of Blue Rock Springs is misaligned.

The other potential Zodiac event that does not align well with a solstice or equinox is the disappearance and apparent murder of Donna Lass, which happened on September 6, 1970, some two and a half weeks before the autumnal equinox. One issue that may be a factor in this case is the distance between San Francisco and Lake Tahoe. With a drive time in the neighborhood of five hours, the Zodiac may have opted to compromise the timing of the crime in the interest of improving other logistical aspects. In particular, Donna Lass disappeared over Labor Day weekend in 1970. Perhaps the additional day of vacation afforded the killer some degree of comfort in perpetrating the crime. Another possibility is that the killer traveled to Lake Tahoe with the intention of only planning the crime, but once there, he decided to go through with it.

A strange curiosity involving the Lass disappearance is the *Chronicle*'s coverage of the story. Prior to moving to Lake Tahoe, Lass had been a resident of San Francisco and had worked as a nurse at Letterman General Hospital in the Presidio. Undoubtedly partially motivated by this connection, the *Chronicle* ran a story about Lass's disappearance three weeks after the fact.[5] That story ran on September 26, just three days after the autumnal equinox. Is it too much of a stretch to entertain the possibility that the killer may have attempted to orchestrate the timing of the Bay Area coverage? Probably. Nevertheless, he likely derived some amount of satisfaction based on the way events played out.

What are we to make of the two celestial events that are completely unaccounted for? The first observation is that the omissions bookend the killer's activity. The first omission occurs immediately after the Zodiac's initial attack. The second omission happens just before his final communiqués. These occurrences suggest a type of ramp-up and cooldown period in the killer's commitment to his persona. The next section will proffer a possible explanation for the ramp-up omission, in other words, why the killer may not have been ready to act a short three months after the Lake Herman Road murders.

As for the Zodiac's omission of the 1970 winter solstice, it's probably the result of the particular transformation that the man made from being an active killer to an inactive one. In other words, the evolving psychodynamics of the killer's troubled mind eventually led him to a point where he abandoned the Zodiac persona. Undoubtedly, this abandonment was not instantaneous. The man did not simply wake up one day and decide to renounce all of his wrongdoing. Rather, he almost certainly went through a gradual conversion over a period of time. Likely, this change was partially governed by the natural progression of the particular mental illness that afflicted him. As speculated later in *The Zodiac Revisited, Volume 3,* Section 2.19, professional psychiatric help may have also played a role. In any event, it's a perfectly logical conclusion that the killer may have felt an inconsistent commitment to his criminal persona during the time frame of his final actions.

Many people are quick to point out each and every imperfection with the idea that the killer was attempting to act in accordance with the solstices and equinoxes, dismissing the possibility as just another one of the wild ideas that the case seems to engender so well. While it's wise to think critically about such proposals and consider them from several different angles, it's also important to keep the various elements of the case in proper perspective. After all, the man who was the Zodiac was just that, a man. And being a man, he was subject to all of the frailties that we human beings know all too well. Moreover, this man was almost certainly a psychopath and was possibly suffering from other mental aberrations as well. It's simply unreasonable to employ a standard where we dismiss this idea because the killer was unable to adhere to it perfectly or his commitment to the idea fluctuated over the course of two-plus years. If we were to employ this same standard to other people pursuing other endeavors, surely many would fail to execute perfectly or have times when their commitment waned during a two-year period. So why is it appropriate to reserve this standard for a mentally-ill serial killer, of all people?

The facts of the matter are: (a) there is strong evidence that the killer called himself the Zodiac based on the concept as it relates to celestial navigation, (b) the solstices and equinoxes are part of the definition of this concept, and (c) there is an important correlation between the timing of many of the Zodiac's actions and the solstices and equinoxes. These facts are exceptionally compelling, and the imperfection of data collected over a two-year time frame is insufficient to negate them. A similar argument regarding imperfection will apply to forthcoming aspects of the proposed methodology.

It's also important to point out that by suggesting the killer was compelled to act on or near the dates of the solstices and equinoxes, I do not mean to say that he necessarily forbade himself from acting at other times as well. Likely, the killer initially intended to commit acts of murder on or near the celestial events. Later, however, after he had established his letter-writing behavior, he was willing to substitute the mailing of a communiqué for the act of murder, as was the case with the Belli Letter near the 1969 winter solstice and the Peek Through the Pines Card (and also the *Los Angeles Times* Letter) near the 1971 spring equinox. Of course, the evidence makes it clear that the man was willing to write letters at any time. He probably preferred only to commit his murders in accordance with the solstices and equinoxes, but as the homicide of Paul Stine shows, he was willing to be flexible on this point also.

3.2.3.1   Evil from Darkness Theme

There is an interesting bit of potential symbolism lurking in the killer's use of the winter solstice. The solstice occurs on the shortest day of the year. The days leading up to the winter solstice get shorter and shorter whereas the days following the solstice get longer and longer. Consequently, the night of the solstice is the longest night of the year. In a symbolic sense, we can think of this night as the height of darkness. By choosing to begin his campaign of murder at the time of the winter solstice, symbolically his persona — the Zodiac — came to life during the height of darkness, so in essence, this darkness spawned the evil that was the Zodiac.

Of course, it took the killer an additional eight months to take credit for the Lake Herman Road murders and to publicly refer to himself as the Zodiac. However, these facts matter little. The key point is that these murders represent the first actions that would later be associated with the Zodiac, and, hence, amount to the birth of the persona.

This idea suggests that the killer may have chosen to wait for the winter solstice before committing his first criminal actions under the guise of his new persona. Depending on when the man decided to commit to becoming the Zodiac, he may have waited several months to a year. On the other hand, from the opposite perspective, these constraints might also help explain some of the timing involved. In particular, the killer may not have been fully prepared to begin his new criminal endeavors, yet he may have felt compelled to act with the arrival of the winter solstice since it only happens once a year. If he was in such a state of unpreparedness, it could explain why he acted at the time of the winter solstice but apparently failed to act during the 1969 spring equinox and why it took him roughly eight months to write his first letters.

3.2.3.2 The Dare

The one crime that does appear to avoid alignment with any solstice or equinox is the murder of Paul Stine. This fact raises the question: why did the killer choose to act differently in this instance? If we search the time frame between the Lake Berryessa attack and Paul Stine's murder, looking for stimuli that may have goaded the killer into action outside of his apparent methodology, one newspaper headline stands out as a real possibility.

On Tuesday, September 30, 1969, the *Examiner* ran a major headline — notably, the killer's first headline in the Bay Area — that was nothing short of a provocative challenge to the Zodiac: "Police Dare Cipher Killer."[6] In the story, Napa County Sheriff's Captain Don Townsend revealed the message that had been written on Bryan Hartnell's car door at the time of the Berryessa attack, with the exception of the final line "by knife," which was being withheld. From the story:

> *And Sheriff's Capt. Don Townsend in effect "dared" him to write or phone again; to prove it.*
>
> *...*
>
> *We are holding back part of the note because, when and if he writes, he can say what else was written there — and thus prove he is the man who 'loves to kill'.*

Of course, the killer never accepted the dare in terms of writing to explicitly identify the phrase that had been withheld.* But given the Zodiac's ego and his level of narcissism, it would have been difficult for the man to have completely ignored such a bold challenge that had been so publicly and so unambiguously thrown down. A short week and a half later, the killer entered Paul Stine's taxicab with the intent to kill. And the following day he did write, identifying himself as the man who murdered Paul Stine as well as being "the same man who did in those people in the north bay area." Perhaps this amounted to his acceptance of the dare. Moreover, perhaps it helps to explain why the killer felt compelled to act in violation of his previously established patterns.

3.2.3.3   Murder Velocity

While we're on the subject of the timing surrounding the murder of Paul Stine, there is another, complementary, possibility that may help explain why the Zodiac chose to act when he did. This idea is something I refer to as "murder velocity." To put it bluntly, in order for the killer to achieve the level of attention he so desperately craved, he needed to act in a way that would put him on par with competing issues of the day.

The Zodiac reached the height of his impact during the latter half of 1969. This time frame was a very tumultuous one for the United States in general and San Francisco in particular. Because of the evolving dynamics that have played out since the Zodiac era, people tend not to associate San Francisco with excessive violence. However, during 1969, the City by the Bay had a notably high per capita murder rate. In fact, on August 7 — a short week after the Zodiac's initial letters — the *Examiner* published an article lamenting the extreme murder rate; the author began by declaring: "This is murder year in San Francisco."[7]

---

*One could argue that Halloween Card, which the killer sent over a year later, was a belated, albeit indirect, acceptance of the dare.

Figure 3.5: The Zodiac's first headline was published in the September 30, 1969, edition of the *San Francisco Examiner*. This headline and its accompanying story may have played a role in motivating the Zodiac to act at an unexpected time. Reproduced with permission of the *San Francisco Examiner*.

At the time of the article, there had been 95 homicides committed in the city since the start of the year. This rate calculates out to one murder every 0.43 days, 3.0 murders per week, 13.0 per month, and 158 per year. Clearly, these are substantial numbers. For better or worse, the people of San Francisco must have grown accustomed to receiving news about the murder of their fellow citizens. Furthermore, other sensational and national news stories were vying for the attention of San Francisco's residents. Noteworthy examples include other instances of serial murder such as Charles Manson and John Norman Collins, as well as the fact that American soldiers were dying in Vietnam at a rate of approximately 100 per week.[8,9]

Therefore, if we take the Zodiac's methodology as it appears to have been originally conceived and give him the benefit of the doubt in terms of his ability to carry it out, he would have acted four times a year and presumably, on each occasion, murdered a couple. Under this scenario, the killer's expected murder rate translates into eight victims per year. To be sure, anyone charged with the protection of a city's population would view a serial killer who murders eight people per year to be an undeniable threat worthy of considerable attention. However, at the same time, when the city in question is experiencing murders at a rate of 158 per year, that same serial killer becomes but a small part of a substantially larger problem.

Now let's consider how the Zodiac's impact changes as a result of Paul Stine's murder. With the Lake Berryessa and Presidio Heights attacks happening just two weeks apart, the killer's murder rate over this time frame is one victim per week which we can extrapolate to fifty-two murders a year. Moreover, if we accept Bryan Hartnell as a victim — given that he was extremely lucky to have survived — the potential murder rate jumps up to seventy-eight per year. When compared against a baseline murder rate of eight, these new murder rates represent an increase of 550–875 percent. Extreme numbers like these are impossible to ignore.

Clearly, the Zodiac could not have, and indeed did not, sustain this impossibly high murder rate. In fact, as far as we know, the slaying of Paul Stine was the last murder that can definitely be attributed to the Zodiac. Nevertheless, the killer's decision to act outside of what appears to be his otherwise communicated pattern undoubtedly was a key reason why he was able to achieve such a high level of impact. Add to these circumstances the other elements of unpredictability that were part of Paul Stine's murder or its aftermath — such as the crime scene location in San Francisco proper and the killer's psychopathic willingness to threaten schoolchildren — and one can easily see how, in a matter of a few days, the Zodiac transformed himself from general Bay Area curiosity to the most-wanted fugitive in California, if not the United States.

3.3   Interpreting the Compass Rose

The next step to better understanding the clues left by the Zodiac is to follow the short instruction that the killer gave alongside the modified compass rose that he drew on the Phillips 66 map. Precisely, the instruction read: "0 is to be set to Mag. N." As noted, magnetic north changes both with time and geographic location. Therefore, to follow this instruction we are required to know the value of magnetic north, or the angle of magnetic declination, in the San Francisco Bay Area during the Zodiac era. There are multiple sources from which we can glean this information. However, the fact that San Francisco exists in a coastal bay affords us the opportunity to use a particularly convenient and precise source, namely compass roses from nautical charts of the San Francisco Bay published by the US government.

Today, the publication of accurate nautical information in the United States lies with the Office of Coast Survey, a department of the National Oceanic and Atmospheric Administration (NOAA). One such nautical chart that serves our purpose particularly well is chart number 5535 from 1970.[10] Detailing the entire San Francisco Bay Area, this chart includes four separate compass roses, one of which is shown in Figure 3.6.

Between the four compass roses, the values of magnetic declination range from 17° 0′ E to 17° 15′ E — "E" stands for east and represents a clockwise direction of rotation. Those unfamiliar with magnetic declination may be surprised to learn that the value is so large. Relatedly, the size of the value is precisely why we need an accurate measurement to have a chance of understanding what the killer was attempting to communicate. On the Phillips 66 map, the Zodiac had centered the hand-drawn compass rose on the peak of Mount Diablo. Of course, that position is not precisely represented on the nautical chart. However, this shortcoming matters little. The process of a serial murderer using a methodology to find victims in or around certain geographic locations is inherently less precise than the task of navigating a seagoing vessel. As a consequence, the nature

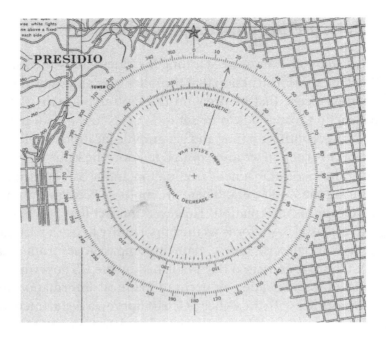

Figure 3.6: One of four compass roses on the 1970 NOAA nautical chart of the San Francisco Bay Area. Coincidentally, the Presidio is identified in the image. Magnetic declination on this compass rose is 17° 15′ E.

of our analysis cannot justify an accuracy beyond that of the nearest degree. Therefore, the compass roses on NOAA chart 5535 indicate we should use a value of 17° E for our magnetic declination.

Using modern computer-based mapping technology, we can start to construct an image that will provide insight into the Zodiac's intended meaning. We begin with the same type of modified compass rose that the killer drew. For the sake of clarity, we modify the compass rose to include the numeric labels that the killer only implied, i.e. 1, 2, 4, 5, 7, 8, 10, and 11. Additionally, we rotate the entire compass rose clockwise 17°, in order to account for the above-described value of magnetic north. Just as the Zodiac had done, we center the image at the precise coordinates of the peak of Mount Diablo. From this point forward, I will refer to this construct as the "rotated compass rose." For the final step, we add the locations of all the killer's definite crime scenes: Lake Herman Road, Blue Rock Springs, Lake Berryessa, and Presidio Heights. The resulting image is shown in Figure 3.7.

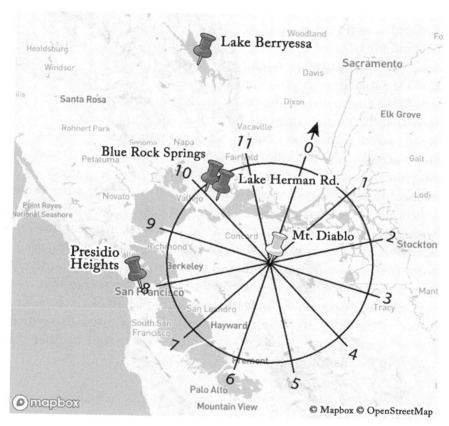

Figure 3.7: The rotated compass rose superimposed on the San Francisco Bay Area with Zodiac crime scene locations noted with pushpins.

A simple inspection of this image reveals some remarkable characteristics. Both of the Vallejo crime scenes exist in a location that aligns exceptionally well with the 10 position of the rotated compass rose. Similarly, Presidio Heights — the one crime scene for which the killer instructed his victim precisely where to go — shows near-perfect alignment with position 8.

Lake Berryessa, the crime scene farthest away from Mount Diablo, shows the least impressive alignment. The nearest position of the rotated compass rose is clearly 11, with a misalignment of approximately 5°. However, the radial line associated with position 11, if appropriately extended, passes through the Monticello Dam at the southeastern tip of the lake. Based on the totality of the evidence, it's possible that the killer allowed himself the flexibility of hunting for victims anywhere along the water's edge of Lake Berryessa given that the radial line for position 11 intersected the body of water.

These alignments of the crime scenes are not coincidental. I believe that the Zodiac, from the birth of his persona on Lake Herman Road, acted within the confines of this methodology. As part of the methodology, the killer chose crime scenes partially based on how they related to the rotated compass rose. For a given crime, I suspect the killer's goal was good alignment with one of the twelve positions. However, there were other aspects of the methodology with which the Zodiac had to contend that further constrained his activity. For this reason, I believe the killer, either eventually or from the beginning, was willing to compromise precise alignment, if necessary, once he had established a set of crime scenes that were well aligned, namely: Lake Herman Road, Blue Rock Springs, and Presidio Heights. In my estimation, the killer viewed these three crime scenes as being sufficient for interested parties to infer this aspect of his methodology.

3.3.1   The *X*'ed Zodiac Symbol

Next, let's examine what I refer to as the *X*'ed Zodiac symbol, shown in Figure 3.8.

The killer drew this relatively large figure at the end of the six-page Bus Bomb Letter that was postmarked November 9, 1969. A close inspection of this figure reveals that, in addition to marking each of the *X*'ed positions, the Zodiac also added small tick marks to each of the unmarked, 30° intervals. Given this segmentation, we

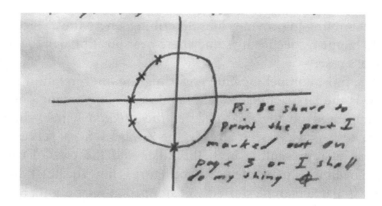

Figure 3.8: The *X*'ed Zodiac symbol with all 30° positions identified and a subset of them called out

can recognize the figure as a representation of the rotated compass rose, even though this figure predates the Phillips 66 map by approximately seven months.

Of course, the most significant characteristic of this figure, from the perspective of our analysis, is that the killer has marked positions 8, 10, and 11 — precisely the positions we determined to be associated with the killer's definite crime scenes in the previous section. Somewhat puzzlingly, the Zodiac also marked off positions 6 and 9. The meaning of one of these two positions can be inferred from the writings of the Zodiac; the other yields no such satisfaction.

3.3.1.1 Position 6

The arrival of the *X*'ed Zodiac symbol coincides with the beginning of the killer's protracted fixation on attempting to convince law enforcement and the public that he intended to blow up a school bus with children on board. Many have argued that the killer never had any such intention and that the entire ordeal was orchestrated purely for the purposes of garnering more attention, terrorizing the public, and wasting law enforcement resources. That debate notwithstanding, the evidence embodied within the killer's letters suggest that he was attempting to provide clues describing where the alleged attack would happen, specifically somewhere near position 6 of the rotated compass rose.

The most compelling clue regarding the interpretation of position 6 is the large Zodiac symbol and its accompanying postscript that appeared on the final page of the *Mikado* Letter, shown in Figure 3.9. As we've seen already, the Zodiac symbol serves a dual purpose of representing both the killer and the rotated compass rose. The first point of interest in the figure is how the killer drew the circle. In particular, he started and stopped at the bottom, precisely the location that corresponds to position 6 on the rotated compass rose. Informally, this is an awkward way to draw a circle. In fact, if we were to ask a large number of people to simply draw a circle, I'm comfortable suggesting that almost nobody would do it this way. Moreover, the killer himself drew a multitude of circles across the collection of his written communications. Yet, this circle is the only instance where he discernibly started and stopped at the bottom of the circle. This characteristic is unnatural, it's explicit, and it's meaningful.

Next, the entire postscript — a statement regarding the "Mt. Diablo code" that allegedly indicates "where the bomb is set" — is centered on position 6. The killer could have placed the postscript anywhere — below the symbol, above the symbol, squeezed into a corner as was the case in Figure 3.8, etc. He explicitly chose to center the text on position 6. Again, this is a meaningful choice.

Given the starting location of the circle and the centering of the text, it's clear that the killer was trying to draw attention to position 6 of the Zodiac symbol, or more accurately the rotated compass rose. In fact, given these two clues and the explicit nature of the hint given in the postscript — which is the only time the killer tried to help people interpret what he meant — there is a nearly palpable sense of desperation on this final page of the letter. The killer is clearly frustrated that nobody has been able to decipher the meaning of his cryptic messages.

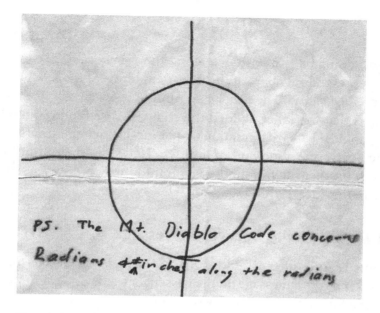

Figure 3.9: The important spatial positioning of the postscript and the telltale starting position of the circle on the final page of the *Mikado* Letter

Both of these ways of emphasizing position 6 utilize a technique that the killer used on multiple occasions. Specifically, he's communicating information by the way he positions words or figures. These are clues — statements of sorts — neither rooted in what's written nor how it's written, but rather where it's placed and how it's positioned relative to other elements on the page. I refer to these clues as spatial information, and coming up, we'll see more of it.

In Section 5.2.5.1, I will discuss a possible solution to the 32 cipher that further supports and otherwise complements the idea that the bomb is associated with position 6 of the rotated compass rose.

3.4   The Quadrant Theory

As intriguing as the positions along the rotated compass rose are, they represent only part of the picture in terms of the killer's apparent methodology. The other key component, as the evidence suggests, is that the killer divided the compass rose (and indirectly his geographic theater of operation) into four distinct quadrants and assigned each one a method of murder. He would then limit the use of each murder method to the quadrant to which it was assigned. I refer to this idea as the "Quadrant Theory."

3.4.1   The Lake Berryessa Message

As noted earlier, after assaulting Bryan Hartnell and Cecelia Shepard, the killer wrote a message on the passenger's-side door of Bryan's car. The last line of that message was the phrase "by knife."

On first consideration, the killer's decision to use this phrase seems odd. Even if both victims had died immediately and there were no eyewitness accounts of the crime, it would have been obvious that the attack had been committed by knife. The phrase makes as much sense as stating other facts that are also obvious, such as "by a lake" or "tied up." When writing such a short message, why would the killer waste words stating something so blatantly obvious?

The reason why the Zodiac wrote "by knife" is that there is more to the phrase than just its immediate applicability to the Lake Berryessa assaults. The killer is not only stating that the crime was committed by knife, he's saying the fact that the victims were attacked by knife is important. The phrase appears to be obvious because the killer is taking an overt detail and pointing out that it is meaningful. The Zodiac wants to make sure that the reader of the message is paying attention to the fact that the crime was committed by knife.

And the meaning of the phrase? It has to do with the killer's methodology. The Zodiac is indicating that something about the crime and his methodology compelled him to attack by knife. This was not a choice made lightly. All of the planning associated with the attack — including the precut lengths of rope, the manipulative cover story, the use of a gun to control the victims — was done specifically to enable an attack that was ultimately perpetrated using a knife. Shooting the victims or killing them through any other means would not have been a satisfactory outcome for the Zodiac. He needed to use a knife because that was the element of his methodology that he wanted to satisfy.

3.4.2   The Halloween Card

If we look through the remainder of the evidence in the case of the Zodiac and consider each piece in terms of how it might relate to a murder-weapon aspect of the methodology, one item stands alone: the Halloween Card.

The back of this greeting card provides two critical pieces of information in terms of understanding the killer's methodology. First, the four methods of murder to which the killer is constraining himself are plainly enumerated: by fire, by gun, by knife, and by rope. And, of course, the phrase "by knife" is exactly what the killer had written on Bryan's car door more than a year before the arrival of the Halloween Card, which further strengthens the association between the Lake Berryessa attack and the communiqué.

The other insight regarding the back of the Halloween Card involves more spatial information. As shown in Figure 3.10, by dividing the back of the card into four quadrants through the use of the intersecting words "PARADICE" and "SLAVES," and then placing one method of murder in each of the four resulting quadrants, the killer is symbolizing how each method is associated with exactly one quadrant. On the card, the killer is simply dividing up the area of the card. In his methodology, however, the quadrants correspond to the rotated compass rose, directly, and indirectly to the killer's geographic theater of operation.

Figure 3.10: The back of the Halloween Card where the Zodiac enumerated four methods of murder, each in its own quadrant. Image reproduced with permission from the *San Francisco Chronicle* / Polaris.

3.4.3   Mapping the Quadrants

Now that we know what the killer was doing, let's compare the quadrants of the rotated compass rose and his assigned murder weapons and see how they stack up with the actual crimes.

Of the four quadrants, the one labeled "by gun" is the easiest to map. Three of the four crimes undoubtedly attributed to the Zodiac were committed using a gun. As the analysis of the rotated compass rose illustrated, the two Vallejo crimes aligned with position 10 and the murder of Paul Stine in Presidio Heights aligned with position 8. Therefore, we can conclude that positions 8 through 10 fall within the "by gun" quadrant.

On first thought we might expect that the killer would assign the quadrants using a subset of the radial lines as boundaries. In other words, the rotated compass rose is divided into twelve slices, each bounded by one of the lines numbered 0 through 11. Perhaps the killer assigned slices 0–2 to one quadrant, 3–5 to the next, and so on. The problem with this approach, however, is that it necessarily requires four of the positions lie on quadrant boundaries. For example, if the line associated with position 3 is used to separate one quadrant from another, and the killer decides to align a crime with position 3, which quadrant would he choose? For this reason, and because the evidence supports the conclusion, the quadrants are not divided along the radial lines associated with the positions, but rather each of the transitions from one quadrant to another happens between two radial lines.

The "by knife" quadrant is nearly as easy to identify in that the Zodiac explicitly spelled out that the Lake Berryessa attack was "by knife." Given that the killer marked off position 11 on the *X*'ed Zodiac symbol, we can infer that the killer was associating the crime with this position, despite its less than perfect alignment. From these circumstances we can infer that the quadrants transition from "by gun" to "by knife" between positions 10 and 11 on the Zodiac's compass rose. A reasonable point of speculation is that the killer would have aligned the quadrants such that the transition happens halfway between the two neighboring positions.

Finally, the killer used significant spatial information to associate position 6 with the bus bomb that he was allegedly building. As an incendiary device, this method of attack would have to belong to the "by fire" quadrant. Therefore, we can label the quadrant in which position 6 exists "by fire." By process of elimination, we assign "by rope" to the remaining quadrant. Pulling all of this information together, Figure 3.11 shows the rotated compass rose with the assigned quadrants.

Apart from satisfying the requirement that quadrants transition between the radial lines associated with the positions, this assignment is also logical in that each quadrant is centered around one of

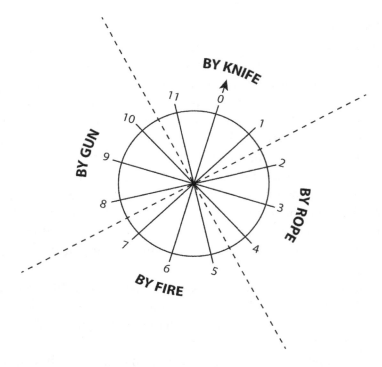

Figure 3.11: The rotated compass rose with the mapped quadrants labeled

the cardinal directions — north, east, south, and west — properly adjusted for magnetic declination, of course. Despite being a bit complex, the layout is very logical.

3.4.4   The Halloween Card Symbol

The formulation of this Quadrant Theory also provides us with a probable explanation for the unusual symbol that the killer drew both inside the Halloween Card and on its accompanying envelope. In particular, the two primary lines of the symbol form a 90° angle. The Zodiac likely intended this angle to represent one of the four quadrants that he otherwise enumerated on the card. In fact, the Halloween Card seems to embody a real sense of desperation on the part of the killer; he is trying exceptionally hard to get the recipient — Paul Avery, whom he knows is familiar with all the details of the case — to understand the importance of the quadrants. Between the explicit depiction of the quadrants on the back of the card, the crisscrossing of words on the inside of the card's envelope, and the two quadrant symbols there are four different references to the idea of quadrants in this single piece of correspondence. Really, the only significant restraint the author demonstrated in communicating his message was changing the order of the enumerated quadrants on the back of the card when compared to the inferred order found on the rotated compass rose.

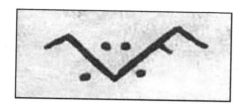

Figure 3.12: The symbol that the Zodiac drew in two places on the Halloween card he sent to Paul Avery

Furthermore, the dots in and around the quadrant symbol are likely associated with a subset of the radial lines from the killer's rotated compass rose. Since there is only one quadrant that has multiple radial positions represented on the X'ed Zodiac symbol, we can infer that the primary quadrant depicted by the symbol is the gun quadrant. To further illustrate this point, Figure 3.13 shows the dotted quadrant symbol superimposed over the X'ed Zodiac symbol with the primary lines positioned to align with the previously identified gun quadrant. As can be seen from this figure, the dots corresponding to positions 6 and 11 are slightly offset from each other to account for their relative spatial location.

Some may quibble about the precise alignment of the dots in positions 8 and 10 or some other slight imperfection. The key point to remember here is that this idea is an abstraction. The killer did

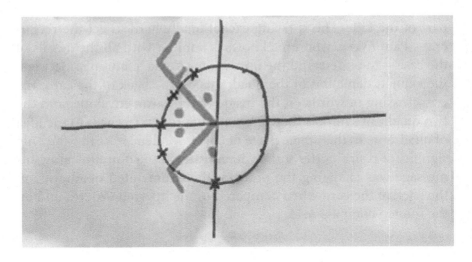

Figure 3.13: The dotted quadrant symbol superimposed over the X'ed Zodiac symbol. The dots correspond to radial positions 6, 8, 10, and 11 — all four of which the Zodiac accounted for by X'ing appropriately.

not create the two figures by superimposing them and methodically aligning all elements to be exactly consistent. Moreover, the X'ed Zodiac symbol was a rather large figure, taking up approximately a quarter of a page. This additional space provided the opportunity for an increased level of precision, although the figure was clearly hand drawn. On the other hand, the dotted quadrant symbol was considerably smaller, and, consequently, the alignment of the dots is more approximate. Nevertheless, the Zodiac still managed to convey the essence of the information.

3.4.5 Position 9?

The one question not answered by the foregoing argument is: why is there an X at position 9 of the X'ed Zodiac symbol? The Quadrant Theory accounts for all the Xs marked by the Zodiac on this clue except for the one at position 9.

As unsatisfying as it may be, I have to suggest that the X at position 9 was likely nothing more than a bit of gamesmanship on the part of the killer. In the same way that he continually referred to an ever-increasing tally of his murders — which was clearly inflated — this errant X amounts to a claim of responsibility for a crime that neither the Zodiac nor anyone else committed.

In fact, the killer constructed the X'ed Zodiac symbol at the same time that he started the practice of adding a running tally to his missives.* The tally at the time of the X'ed Zodiac symbol was seven, which was two more than his known victim count. Therefore, when constructing this spatial representation of his victims, perhaps the Zodiac felt compelled to throw in an additional X to represent another crime scene to account for his exaggerated number of victims. Of particular note, the dotted quadrant symbol from the Halloween Card does *not* have a dot associated with position 9; this omission supports the idea that position 9 does not correspond to an actual Zodiac crime.

3.4.6 Reconsidering the Zodiac Symbol

Now that we understand the concepts of the zodiac circle and the rotated compass rose, especially with respect to the above-described methodology, we can begin to view the killer's chosen symbol, $\oplus$, as an abstraction that conveys meaning on multiple different levels. As noted earlier, it can be thought of as an abbreviation for the full zodiac circle. However, in light of the killer's commingling of the zodiac circle and the compass rose, we can also think of the symbol as a representation of the Zodiac's rotated compass rose, as it relates to his methodology. In fact, by abbreviating the rotated compass rose with only two lines that represent the four cardinal directions, the killer is further symbolizing and emphasizing the quadrant aspect of

---

*The X'ed Zodiac symbol appeared at the end of the Bus Bomb Letter which was postmarked November 9, 1969. The first instance of the killer using a murder tally was on the Dripping Pen Card, postmarked one day earlier.

his methodology. In other words, the symbol can be thought of as a representation of the killer's geographic theater of operation with each quadrant centered around one of the four cardinal directions.

Clearly, this symbol was not conceived in haste. Although graphically simple, the symbolic construct has multiple layers of meaning, and, therefore, we can deduce that it was important to the killer. Just as he would not have been satisfied with any name other than the Zodiac, so too it was important to him that his public persona be represented by this self-assigned symbol.

3.4.7   A Telling Choice of Words

As recounted in Section 3.1 of *The Zodiac Revisited, Volume 1*, the killer reportedly said "I'm going to have to tie you up" and "I'm going to have to stab you" during the Lake Berryessa attack. These phrases are unusually passive. The man could have said, "I'm going to stab you" or something similar. Instead, he said, "I'm going to *have to* stab you," as if he was being compelled to act by some guiding force. I suggest that this choice of words was actually an acknowledgment — made either consciously or subconsciously — that the killer was driven by a methodology. He *had* to stab Bryan and Cecelia because his methodology required that he stab one or more victims — preferably a couple — in close proximity to Lake Berryessa on or near the weekend of September 27. This commitment left the killer relatively little flexibility in the commission of the crime. Cecelia was murdered and Bryan was gravely injured simply because they had unknowingly satisfied the self-imposed constraints of a murderous psychopath.

3.5   The Benefits of Methodology

Adoption of a methodology such as the one described in the preceding sections is downright bizarre. If examples of similar behavior exist in the history of serial murder, certainly none are so intricate and complicated.

Beyond any psychological need served by the killer's use of this methodology, there is one practical aspect from which the Zodiac has benefited enormously: By allowing his activities to be partially dictated by a set of self-imposed rules, the killer effectively distanced himself from his own actions and, therefore, made it more difficult for law enforcement to gather meaningful information. Furthermore, the rules systematically introduced variables into the killer's behavior that ultimately created confusion for anyone who dared to try to make sense of the case.

For example, much has been made about the cross-jurisdictional nature of the Zodiac case. Those making the argument usually suggest that the involvement of so many different law enforcement agencies led to a lack of communication and sharing of information which, in turn, impeded progress in apprehending the murderer. In my estimation, too much weight is given to this argument. While it certainly is true that handling a case distributed across multiple jurisdictions will be less efficient, there is little evidence to suggest that had the crimes all been committed in the same jurisdiction the killer would have been apprehended.

Nevertheless, the reason that the Zodiac case involved so many law enforcement agencies was due to the killer distributing his crimes across various geographic locations — and that decision was a direct result of the killer's self-imposed methodology.

Another related way in which the geographic nature of the methodology ultimately frustrated efforts to understand the Zodiac has to do with Vallejo. Numerous people have speculated that the Zodiac lived in Vallejo. Usually, proponents point out two facts in making this case. First, the Zodiac's first two attacks happened in Vallejo.* The suggestion is that the killer started locally and then branched out to other areas. The second piece of the argument is that Lake Herman Road and, to a lesser extent, Blue Rock Springs were secluded, lovers' lanes that only local residents would have known about.

---

*Technically, the Zodiac murdered David Faraday and Betty Lou Jensen in Benicia, but the crime scene was just past the Vallejo border.

The question of why the killer chose to strike in two different but nearby locations is not directly answered by the above-described methodology, however, the question of why Lake Herman Road and Blue Rock Springs is obvious: they fit the killer's geographic criteria. To the killer the crime scenes were, first and foremost, points on a map. As a matter of secondary concern, the man looked for areas in which he could find his desired type of victims — ideally couples seeking romantic seclusion. Finally, the locations needed to be accommodating in terms of perpetrating the crimes. By choosing the crime scenes using this ulterior set of requirements, the killer enabled those analyzing his crimes to assign more normal, but ultimately incorrect, motives to his selections.

One of the more interesting developments to have happened in the area of forensic science since the time of the Zodiac's last-known communication is the practice of geographic profiling. Using this technique, investigators analyze a large collection of solved crimes and develop detailed statistical models about the relationship between crime scene locations and perpetrator residence. The software that performs the profiling can then apply this library of statistical information to aid the analysis of unsolved crimes. Specifically, investigators input the coordinates of known crime scenes and the tool can generate what's known as a heat map that indicates the probability that a perpetrator lived in a specific geographical region.

In conjunction with the release of David Fincher's 2007 movie *Zodiac*, the producers enlisted the help of Kim Rossmo, a pioneer in geographic profiling, to apply the technique to the case of the Zodiac. The resulting heat map showed that the killer most likely lived in Vallejo or Benicia. In some sense, we can think of these results as statistical validation of the intuition that led many people to a similar conclusion.

Geographic profiling has proven itself to be a valuable tool for helping law enforcement agencies solve crimes, and investigators from all over the world have been trained in the technique.[11] However, in the case of the Zodiac, I suspect the value of the technique is effectively zero. Why? Because the killer's use of the above-described methodology has defeated it. By specifically employing a set of rules that were created to vary the locations of his crime scenes based on factors that have nothing to do with normal criminal behavior, the killer destroyed the applicability of any geographic profile compiled from normal criminal behavior. While he almost certainly did not devise his methodology with the intention of frustrating future developments in forensic science, he effectively ended up doing just that.

It is well known within the law enforcement community that crimes involving the murder of strangers are some of the most difficult to solve because there is no existing relationship between the perpetrator and victim that investigators can exploit to work backward from the victim to the murderer. In addition to preying on strangers, the Zodiac was further impeding law enforcement's investigative efforts by removing additional elements of his own personality from the formulation of his crimes.

Though there is no question that the Zodiac had more than his fair share of luck, it's also true that his adherence to a criminal methodology played a significant role in enabling the man to evade capture.

Notes

1. Keith Power, "Astrologer Joins Hunt for Killer," *San Francisco Chronicle*, October 17, 1969, 3.

2. Nathaniel Bowditch, *The American Practical Navigator*, Washington: US Naval Oceanographic Office, 1966, p. 374.

3. Bowditch, *American Practical Navigator*, p. 371.

4. Robert Graysmith, *Zodiac*, New York: Berkley Books, 1987.

5. "Nurse Vanishes — A Tahoe Mystery," *San Francisco Chronicle*, September 26, 1970, 3.

6. "Car Door Message Revealed," *San Francisco Examiner*, September 30, 1969, 1.

7. "The City's Map of Murder," *San Francisco Examiner*, August 7, 1969, 6.

8. "Hollywood 'Ritual' Slayings," *San Francisco Sunday Examiner & Chronicle*, August 10, 1969, A1.

9. "Suspect Held in Coed Death," *San Francisco Examiner*, August 1, 1969, 11.

10. Office of Coast Survey, *San Francisco Bay — Chart 5535*, 1970, Accessed November 25, 2020, *http://zodiacrevisited.com/book/noaa-1970-sf-bay*.

11. João Medeiros, "How Geographic Profiling Helps Find Serial Criminals," *Wired*, November 10, 2014, Accessed November 25, 2020, *http://zodiacrevisited.com/book/wired-geographic-profiling*.

4

Crafting a Persona

*... no one reveals himself as he is; we all wear
a mask and play a role.*

Arthur Schopenhauer, German philosopher,
1788–1860

One reasonable and compelling interpretation of the Zodiac saga is that the persona represented an escalation in serial murder. Having killed high school sweethearts Robert Domingos and Linda Edwards as well as newlyweds Joyce and Johnny Ray Swindle, the nascent serial killer felt the satisfaction of preying on those against whom he harbored a deep-seated hatred — namely women and, to a lesser extent, the men who were able to engage in intimate relationships with them. Moving on to Cheri Jo Bates, the killer, for the first time, directed his murderous attention solely at a woman — the primary target of his hatred. With each crime, the killer experienced an increased sense of confidence as he challenged society in general and law enforcement in particular and emerged victorious every time.

By the time the killer murdered Cheri Jo Bates, however, the idea of terrorizing society exclusively through the act of murder was no longer satisfying. Like a drug user developing a tolerance, the man wanted something more; he *needed* something more. In searching for some way to relive the experience and enhance his sense of morbid accomplishment, the killer decided to communicate with the police and the public by writing letters, which he did to great effect via "The Confession." Soon after, he also began tormenting the people directly traumatize by his murderous deeds when he sent a taunting note to Cheri's father, Joseph Bates.

Then sometime between April 1967 and December 1968, the man who would become known as the Zodiac relocated to the San Francisco Bay Area. Still affected by the mental anomaly that compelled him to kill, the murderer saw the move as an opportunity to begin anew. Troubled by the diminishing satisfaction of individual murders and motivated by the excitement of directly corresponding with law enforcement and the public, the man commenced taking his murderous evolution to the next level.

The plan was to orchestrate a campaign of murder and correspondence intended to terrorize the people of the Bay Area. The crimes would all be linked to a single person, or more precisely, a persona. The killer, of course, would remain unknown, but the persona would be known to all, recognizable by an assumed name — a name of the killer's own choosing.

While the adoption of the murderous persona was sufficient to satisfy various aspects of the killer's evolving psychological needs, it was not enough to placate the man's desire to feel superior to law enforcement. For that, the man decided to add another dimension to his alter ego. Not only would he commit his crimes, but he'd commit them in some kind of systematic, methodological manner that, once revealed, would intensify both the public's sense of helplessness and law enforcement's level of frustration.

With these thoughts in mind, the killer began to develop the elements of his murderous persona and his corresponding methodology. His journey eventually led him to become the Zodiac.

4.1 Probable Influences

The persona that we now know as the Zodiac is a complex and multilayered creation. Though some aspects of the killer's alter ego are easily inferable through his actions and behaviors, other aspects offer little in the way of clear meaning — much like the rest of the case. Relatedly, trying to identify material that served as inspiration for the killer when he crafted the persona is a challenge that involves varying degrees of difficulty. In this section, we start by considering subjects that are strongly supported by the evidence.

4.1.1 The Most Dangerous Game

In the deciphered 408 cryptogram, the Zodiac wrote:*

```
I LIKE KILLING PEOPLE BECAUSE IT IS SO
MUCH FUN. IT IS MORE FUN THAN KILLING
WILD GAME IN THE FORREST BECAUSE MAN
IS THE MOST DANGEROUS ANIMAL OF ALL.
```

As many have noted, the notion of man being the "most dangerous" animal or game is clearly a reference to the story "The Most Dangerous Game."[1-3] Given that the killer was moved by the story to the point of referencing it in his writing, it's a subject that deserves our attention.

4.1.1.1 Story Recap

After a mishap at sea, a world-famous hunter named Rainsford finds himself washed ashore the ominously named Shipwreck Island. Having heard the unmistakable sound of a gunshot, Rainsford sets out to find the isle's inhabitants. Before long, he discovers a massive, castle-like dwelling.

---

*Encipherment errors corrected and implied punctuation added.

Shortly thereafter, Rainsford is introduced to the island's primary occupant, Count Zaroff. An aristocrat from formerly czarist Russia, Zaroff is a man of great means who has managed to accommodate the isolated living area with many of the comforts of culture, wealth, and privilege.

Through pleasant and eloquent conversation over an exquisitely prepared meal, Zaroff slowly recounts the events of his life that have led to him inhabiting Shipwreck Island. The count explains that he is first and foremost a hunter. However, a lifetime of big-game hunting ultimately left him unfulfilled due to the inability of any animal to pose a real challenge. Slowly and disturbingly, Zaroff reveals how he has solved his problem by hunting the one prey worthy of his time: man.

Soon after, Rainsford, the world-famous hunter, plays the unfamiliar role of prey as he matches wits with Count Zaroff in a life-and-death game of survival.

4.1.1.2 Context and Analysis

The tale of "The Most Dangerous Game" began life as a short story written by Richard Connell. It was first published in *Collier's Weekly* in 1924; it has also been published under the title "The Hounds of Zaroff." Because of its universally compelling theme of predator turned prey, the short story has been told, retold, adapted, and has otherwise served as inspiration for a plethora of productions across the full spectrum of media, including print, radio, film, and television.

Perhaps the most successful adaptation of the story was the 1932 movie by the same name. Interestingly, the film was made by RKO Studios in parallel with the classic movie *King Kong*. The simultaneous production of the two movies allowed the producers to defray costs by getting twice the mileage out of the cast, crew, and sets. Many of the Shipwreck Island jungle scenes were filmed on sets that later became Skull Island in *King Kong*. Additionally, screenwriter

James Ashmore Creelman took artistic liberties with Connell's original story and added a damsel-in-distress character, Eve, played by
King Kong star Fay Wray.

   Given the relative popularities of the various adaptations of
Connell's story, there is a strong likelihood that this film version
inspired the Zodiac to use the phrase "most dangerous animal"
when he wrote the content of the 408 cipher.

   Interestingly, some of the dialogue at the beginning of *The Most
Dangerous Game* may well have struck a chord with the Zodiac and
further motivated him to make reference to the movie.[4]

Doctor:	*I'll tell you what I had on my mind. I was thinking of the inconsistency of civilization. The beast of the jungle, killing just for his existence, is called savage. The man, killing just for sport, is called civilized.*
Passenger:	*Hear, hear.*
Doctor:	*It's a bit contradictory, isn't it?*
Rainsford:	*Now just a minute. What makes you think it isn't just as much sport for the animal as it is for the man? Now take that fellow right there, for instance. [Rainsford points to a picture of a tiger taken during a recent hunting trip.] There never was a time when he couldn't have gotten away. But he didn't want to. He got interested in hunting me. He didn't hate me for stalking him any more than I hated him for trying to charge me. As a matter of fact, we admired each other.*

   The duality of the predator-turned-prey theme probably resonated with the Zodiac. On the one hand, he was a predator
hunting his victims. On the other hand, he was prey hunted by law
enforcement. More importantly, the killer may well have identified
with this notion of mutual admiration as articulated by Rainsford.
In this sense, the reference to *The Most Dangerous Game* can be

interpreted as an assertion by the killer that he is a worthy opponent, equal with law enforcement and deserving of respect. The Zodiac wanted law enforcement to admire him during their hunt, just as Rainsford admired the tiger.

Of course, in the aftermath of the Stine murder, San Francisco Chief of Inspectors Martin Lee orchestrated a campaign to minimize the public's perception of a threat by characterizing the Zodiac in very unflattering terms, labeling him a clumsy criminal, a liar, and a latent homosexual.[5] Although perhaps less intentionally, other members of law enforcement achieved similar ends through other labels such as "impotent" and "afraid of women."[6] Clearly, any self-imagined perceptions the killer had as an equal adversary deserving of respect and admiration were diametrically opposed to the image that the police were constructing of him.

This discrepancy between the killer's view of how he deserved to be perceived and the reality of the picture law enforcement painted would have represented a significant source of injustice in the mind of the killer. This perceived slight was probably the largest contributing factor to, if not the sole reason for, the changing in the way that the killer interacted with police as described in the Bus Bomb Letter.

4.1.2   Charlie Chan at Treasure Island

As many people over the years have noted, another potential source that probably influenced the killer during the creation of his persona is the movie *Charlie Chan at Treasure Island*.[2,3] Filmed and released in 1939, the movie starred Sidney Toler in the role of world-famous Chinese detective Charlie Chan. A young Cesar Romero — perhaps best known for his later portrayal of the Joker in the movie (1966) and TV series (1966–1968) *Batman* — was cast as the magician Fred Rhadini.

4.1.2.1 Summary

As the movie opens, Charlie and his son Jimmy are flying to San Francisco to attend the International Exposition being held on Treasure Island. Also on board the plane is Paul Essex, one of Charlie's old friends. Paul is an author returning from a working vacation in Hawaii where he has just put the finishing touches on his latest novel.

While talking to Charlie, Paul receives an apparently bothersome radiogram.* Soon after, while the plane prepares to land, Paul is found dead and the contents of the radiogram are revealed:

> SIGN OF SCORPIO INDICATES DISASTER IF
> ZODIAC OBLIGATIONS ARE IGNORED.

In the resulting confusion, Paul's recently completed manuscript disappears.

Once in San Francisco, Charlie quickly meets up with some old friends including Deputy Chief J.J. Kilvaine of the San Francisco Police Department and *San Francisco Chronicle* reporter Pete Lewis. The latter introduces Charlie to Fred Rhadini, a celebrity magician who performs regularly on Treasure Island. Lewis goes on to explain that he and Rhadini are collaborating; specifically, the *Chronicle* is backing Rhadini in an exposé of fake psychics. Soon the conversation turns to "the Great Dr. Zodiac," whom Lewis describes as "the big shot in the spook racket around here."[7]

Through additional plot developments, it is revealed that Dr. Zodiac — who is interchangeably referred to as "Dr. Zodiac" and just "Zodiac" — has accumulated a veritable library of disagreeable information on a massive number of people, and he's using it for blackmail. Furthermore, Dr. Zodiac is implicated in driving several people to commit suicide, including Paul Essex.

---

*A type of 1930s in-flight message

Eventually, Charlie puts the pieces of the puzzle together during a theatrical showdown between Rhadini and Dr. Zodiac. As it turns out, the two are, in fact, one and the same.

4.1.2.2 Context and Analysis

This story buckles under the weight of its efforts to provide a surprise ending. For example, the person who actually is Dr. Zodiac, Rhadini, never appears on screen as Dr. Zodiac. Rather, during the two scenes with Dr. Zodiac, he is being impersonated by a faithful assistant. Add to this a self-inflicted wound and the resolution of the mystery through a "scientific" demonstration of mental telepathy, and it's safe to say the story leaves something to be desired, at least by modern standards. Nevertheless, many consider the film to be Sidney Toler's best as well as one of the better installments of the entire *Charlie Chan* series.

There are some obvious parallels between the movie and the enigmatic killer, in particular, a villain named Zodiac, a setting in San Francisco, and the heavy plot involvement of the *San Francisco Chronicle*. But a certain passage in the dialogue offers even more thought-provoking possibilities. Note that Charlie's broken English is quoted verbatim.

Charlie: *But Dr. Zodiac not ordinary criminal. He is man with great ego with disease known to science as: pseudologia fantastica.*

Pete: *[whistles]*

Jimmy: *Is it serious?*

Charlie: *Listen. [Reading from a book] Pathological liars and swindlers suffer from exaggerated fantasy, unleashed vanity, and great ambition, which robs them of caution known to saner men.*

Jimmy: *Or as Pop would put it: "Swelled head gives owner more trouble than indigestion."*

Charlie: *Correction, please. Swelled head sometimes give police more cooperation than criminal mistake.*

Pete: *Say, I'll buy that. We might trip Zodiac through his vanity.*

Charlie: *Criminal egotist find pleasure in laughing at police.*

This last line aptly describes a fundamental signature element of the Zodiac persona. Moreover, in the very next scene, Dr. Zodiac accepts a challenge put forth by Rhadini, Lewis, and the *Chronicle*. He does so through a note that reads:

I accept your challenge to a demonstration of my powers.
I shall appear on your stage [tonight].

Dr. Zodiac

Of interest in this hand-printed note is the slightly self-important phraseology that would come to be favored by the San Francisco serial killer some forty years later, namely: "I shall."

There is no doubt that coincidence is a real phenomenon that has plagued the case of the Zodiac. Sometimes parts of the evidence that seem undeniably meaningful turn out to be nothing more than remarkable instances of happenstance. Examples of such coincidences are reviewed in Section 4.3 (Noninfluences). Having said that, it's difficult to accept that the ideas found in *Charlie Chan at Treasure Island* played no role in the killer's formation of his murderous alter ego. There are just too many ways in which the elements of the story fit and fit well. Certainly, the killer's persona extends far beyond the boundaries of the film, and, in this sense, the ideas represent more of a starting point than an end. Nevertheless, the probable contribution of the film is a near certainty.

4.1.3　Ko-Ko the Lord High Executioner

On two separate occasions, the Zodiac expressed himself by quoting lines from Ko-Ko, the Lord High Executioner in Gilbert and Sullivan's 1885 comic opera *The Mikado or The Town of Titipu*, usually called simply *The Mikado*. In the first instance, the killer used two and a half pages to transcribe, albeit imperfectly, Ko-Ko's "I've Got a Little List" song from Act I. This lengthy homage comprised the majority of the five-page letter that he sent on June 26, 1970. Because of the content, people often refer to this letter as the *Mikado* Letter or, alternatively, the Little List Letter. Later, the Zodiac again paid tribute to the Ko-Ko character in the 1974 *Exorcist* Letter. In this communiqué, he quoted a much shorter three-line passage of the song *Willow, Tit-willow* from Act II, near the end of the opera.

4.1.3.1　The Ko-Ko Symbolism

To fully understand why the Ko-Ko character may have appealed to the Zodiac, we must delve into the opera. Near the beginning of the story, a noble lord named Pish-Tush provides some background about the Mikado, also known as the emperor of Japan:

> *Our great Mikado, virtuous man,*
> *When he to rule our land began,*
> *Resolved to try*
> *A plan whereby*
> *Young men might best be steadied.*
> *So he decreed, in words succinct,*
> *That all who flirted, leered, or winked*
> *(Unless connubially linked),*
> *Should forthwith be beheaded.*

Unfortunately, this well-intentioned decree had some regrettable consequences. Pish-Tush continues:

This stern decree, you'll understand,
Caused great dismay throughout the land!
For young and old
And shy and bold
Were equally affected.
The youth who winked a roving eye,
Or breathed a non-connubial sigh,
Was thereupon condemned to die —
He usually objected

Finally, Pish-Tush explains how the powers that be in Titipu solved the problem:

And so we straight let out on bail
A convict from the county jail,
Whose head was next
On some pretext
Condemned to be mown off,
And made him Headsman, for we said,
"Who's next to be decapited
Cannot cut off another's head
Until he's cut his own off!"

Of course, the convict was Ko-Ko. Soon after, dialogue between two other characters provides some additional context.

Nanki-Poo: *Ko-Ko, the cheap tailor, Lord High Executioner of Titipu! Why, that's the highest rank a citizen can attain!*

Pooh-Bah: *It is. Our logical Mikado, seeing no moral difference between the dignified judge who condemns a criminal to die and the industrious mechanic who carries out the sentence, has rolled the two offices into one, and every judge is now his own executioner.*

Through this character development, we can see a symbolism that may well have resonated with the Zodiac. Ko-Ko is promoted to the exalted rank of Lord High Executioner, whereby society empowers him to serve as judge and executioner. Principal among his duties is the imposition of the death penalty for anyone found guilty of flirting outside marriage. Since the Zodiac preferred to prey on young couples seeking romantic isolation, he almost certainly viewed himself as a modern-day Ko-Ko, passing judgment on such couples and administering his own form of capital punishment. This perception would have been consistent with the killer's exaggerated sense of self-importance.

However, this analogy is flawed for a couple of reasons. Whereas Ko-Ko was vested with his power via the society in which he lived, the source of the Zodiac's perceived legitimacy came from the seeds of jealousy cultivated in the fertile soil of mental illness. Moreover, the Ko-Ko character is fundamentally a nonviolent person. To be sure, he's happy to be the beneficiary of his improbable circumstances. Yet he has much more in common with the people doing the flirting than the people who truly want to see the flirters put to death. For these reasons, as well as the circumstances that led to him being chosen for the position, he never acts to fulfill his duties as Lord High Executioner. Even when Ko-Ko's substantial troubles would simply vanish if he were to execute a happily obliging participant, he's forced to exclaim: "I can't kill anything! I can't kill anybody!" In fact, this element of the story — a Lord High Executioner who cannot kill anybody — is a fundamental part of the farcical tale. Nevertheless, the overt ways in which the Ko-Ko symbolism works overshadows the more subtle ways in which it does not.

4.1.3.2   I've Got a Little List

Regardless of the details surrounding the Zodiac's perception of Ko-Ko as a kindred spirit, there is little doubt that the killer found much to like about the lyrics of the song "I've Got a Little List." In this lighthearted musical diatribe from early in the operetta, Ko-Ko bombastically explains that he'll have no problem performing his duties if he's called upon to do so. In particular, he can easily find a victim because he maintains a "little list" of various types of people who annoy him and "might well be underground," a euphemism for dead and buried, of course. Broken up by choruses of "they'll none of 'em be missed," Ko-Ko works his way through his enumeration before arriving at the musical climax where he concludes:

> *But it really doesn't matter whom you put upon the list*
> *For they'd none of 'em be missed — they'd none of 'em be missed*

To those of us existing within the boundaries of societal norms, this song, and *The Mikado* as a whole, is an absurdity whose primary purpose is to entertain. But the Zodiac undoubtedly had a different perspective. As a psychopath actually engaged in selecting victims whom he intended to kill, he surely related to the lyrics in a more practical sense. Furthermore, given the remorselessness the killer exhibited — for example his callousness in discussing his victims and his willingness to threaten innocent and helpless schoolchildren — there is little question that he maintained an attitude similar to the conclusion of the song, that it really just didn't matter whom he killed.

In the investigation following the arrival of the *Mikado* Letter, detectives theorized that the numerous mistakes in the lyrics indicated that the killer had re-created the stanzas from memory instead of copying them. This line of reasoning led to speculation that the man may have played the role of Ko-Ko in a production of the opera. Interestingly, police questioned several men who had formerly taken the stage as the character.[8] Not surprisingly, they were all cleared.

One notable aspect of the song "I've Got a Little List" is that its lyrics have been in a constant state of evolution. For example, the line:

> *There's the banjo serenader, and the others of his race*

originally included the offensive racial slur "There's the nigger serenader..." As cultural norms shifted and the word became unacceptable, productions made the change. Because the Zodiac used the word "banjo," we can be sure he was basing his content on a production that happened sometime after 1948.[9]

Similarly, there are other lines in the song that have also changed over time, although often for less identifiable reasons. As another example, there was a 1967 film version of *The Mikado* that, timing wise, seems as if it could have been a likely candidate to have influenced the Zodiac, even though people at the time did not have a way to easily re-watch movies that had completed their theatrical runs. Regardless, we can exclude this version of the opera from being the basis of the killer's lyrical homage because it has Gilbert's original line:

And that singular anomaly, the lady novelist

instead of the one found in the Zodiac's letter:

And that singular anomaly, the girl who's never kissed

In fact, this line is an especially good clue since most readily available productions from the mid-twentieth century favor either the original line or one where "lady novelist" is replaced by "prohibitionist." Although there were productions that used the line "the girl who's never kissed," it was a much less common choice.

If we consider the specifics of the lyrics that the Zodiac wrote and compare them with known versions of *The Mikado* that the killer may have used as a reference when crafting his letter, there's really only one known production that survives this test of scrutiny: the audio recording of the 1960, *Bell Telephone Hour* performance. Columbia Records released this LP* to coincide with the April 29, 1960 airing of the performance on NBC.[10-12] Interestingly, this installment of *The Mikado* featured a near retirement-age Groucho Marx in the role of Ko-Ko. Though you might expect the audio recording to be an exact

---

*Zodiac researcher Misty Johansen played an instrumental role in identifying this audio recording as a likely source of Zodiac inspiration and advocating for its importance.

re-creation of the broadcast audio, there were noticeable differences between the two. Of particular note, the television version of "I've Got a Little List" omitted the entire second verse; the LP did not. Hence, it is the LP version, and only the LP version, that matches the lyrical content of the Zodiac's letter.

Moreover, the use of this recording also explains how the author managed to include every line of the libretto but still made so many mistakes in the words themselves. The medium provides the answer. The killer didn't copy the words directly, nor had he recalled them from memory — as detectives had theorized — but, rather, he transcribed the content by listening to the recording.

Though helpful in terms of better understanding the killer, this scenario still leaves open the question: how are we to interpret the numerous mistakes penned by the author during his transcription? Examples of these mistakes are shown in Figure 4.1.

*There's the **pestilential nuisances who write** for autographs*
*There is the **pestulentual nucences who whrite** for autographs*

*All children who are up in dates, and **floor you with 'em flat***
*All children who are up in dates and **implore you with implatt***

*And all third persons who **on spoiling tête-à-têtes insist***
*And all third persons who **with unspoiling take thoes who insist***

*And the people who eat **peppermint and puff** it in your face*
*All people who eat **pepermint and phomphit** in your face*

*And that **Nisi Prius nuisance**, who just now is rather rife*
*And that **nice impriest** that is rather rife*

Figure 4.1: Examples of transcription errors made by the killer. In each case, the correct line is given, followed by the Zodiac's version.

As is evident from these examples, there's a substantial range in the severity of the mistakes that the killer made in his transcription. Many of us without preexisting knowledge of the Latin phrase "Nisi Prius" would fail the task of accurately transcribing it. On the other hand, hearing "puff it in your face" as "phomphit in your face" feels improbable, if not contrived.

In the end, how one feels about these inaccuracies is probably a reflection of how one interprets the larger and often-disputed question of the Zodiac's frequent spelling mistakes. Those who feel the killer's inability to spell is an accurate indication of his language skills are sure to conclude that the errors in "I've Got a Little List" are just more of the same. Similarly, those of us who attribute the Zodiac's spelling woes to deceptive manipulation also will view the lyrical missteps as more of the same. The only caveat in the latter case involves the additional variable of transcription. Under this scenario, the killer may well have known some of the words and simply chosen to mistranscribe them. For others, however, he may not have been able to tell what was being said. But, since his intention was to misrepresent his language proficiency anyway, he probably didn't try very hard to figure it out and, instead, simply replaced any difficult-to-transcribe passage with something that sounded phonetically similar.

4.1.3.3   Other *Mikado* Observations

The Zodiac's quoting of the song "Willow, Titwillow" is important because of its suicide symbolism, as described in the discussion of the *Exorcist* Letter in Section 2.17 of *The Zodiac Revisited, Volume 3*. But beyond that, there's not much more to say about it. It's short, predictably imperfect, and that's about it.

There is, however, another reference to *The Mikado* besides the two more or less direct quotes from Ko-Ko the Lord High Executioner. On page 2 of the *Mikado* Letter, at the end of his torture-laden victim fantasy, the Zodiac writes the following, almost as a precursor to the direct but imperfect quoting of "I've Got a Little List":

And
all billiard players I shall
have them play in a dark
ened dungon cell with crooked
cues + Twisted Shoes.

This too is a reference to *The Mikado*, but not a direct one. It's adapted from "A More Humane Mikado," the famous "let the punishment fit the crime" song sung by the Mikado character himself. The relevant lines of Gilbert's* original libretto — which the 1960 LP version reproduced faithfully — are (emphasis added):

*The **billiard**-sharp whom anyone catches*
His doom's extremely hard —
He's made to dwell
*In a **dungeon cell***
On a spot that's always barred.
And there he plays extravagant matches
In fitless finger-stalls,
On a cloth untrue
*With a **twisted cue***
And elliptical billiard balls.

As we can see, this reference is much more flawed, for example, "on a cloth untrue with a twisted clue" becomes "with crooked cue + twisted shoes." Nonetheless, it's still obviously derived from the lyrical imagery. Here the killer is, perhaps, adapting to his own content and, therefore, simply unconcerned with faithful reproduction. Or, alternatively, this result may have been a combination of inaccurately recalling the lines from memory and further modifying them. Whatever the case, it's a substantially different scenario from the other references to *The Mikado*.

---

*Gilbert wrote the libretto; Sullivan composed the music.

4.2　Possible Influences

For a couple of the ideas that may have influenced the killer during the creation of his Zodiac persona, we lack enough evidence to label them as probable. Nevertheless, they are not only possible but also intriguing.

4.2.1　Japanese Maps

There is a fascinating possibility lurking in the evidence of the Zodiac case. To expose it, we start by noting a Japanese theme in some of the Zodiac's writing. With dragons being so prevalent in Japanese culture, one could argue that the Dragon Card is an instance of this theme. But the more obvious first occurrence is the killer's just-discussed long-winded channeling of the character Ko-Ko from *The Mikado*, which was set in Japan — albeit a foreigner's arguably flawed view of Japan. Later, the killer continued with the theme in the *Exorcist* Letter, once again quoting Ko-Ko and also augmenting the letter with some unusual symbols that look distinctly Asian, if not Japanese.

　　In the mid-1800s, Western cartographers introduced the idea of the compass rose to their Japanese counterparts who, in turn, immediately began using the concept in their maps. Soon, however, some of these Japanese compass roses adopted their own characteristics. In particular, whereas the Western compass roses from this era were divided into thirty-two evenly spaced directions, the Japanese mapmakers took some artistic liberty and divided theirs into twelve directions. But what is truly fascinating — from our perspective — is the reason that these nineteenth-century mapmakers chose to use twelve directions: they were dividing the compass rose into the twelve signs of the Chinese zodiac.[13]

　　The potential importance of this historical fact is significant. As previously noted, the evidence in the Zodiac case suggests (a) the killer named himself after the celestial zodiac, (b) he was aware of the standard nautical compass rose, (c) he crafted a methodology for

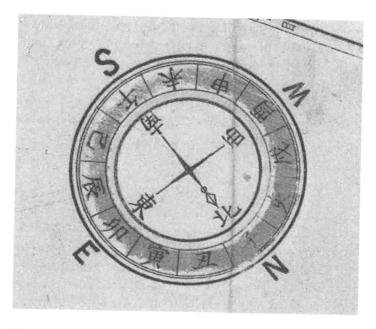

Figure 4.2: An 1885* map of Yokohama, Japan, shows a compass rose divided into twelve equal segments, which is based on the signs of the Chinese zodiac. In this particular map, the cardinal directions are also annotated with letters from the English alphabet. Credit: Hanken menkyo doban Yokohama chizu / Ozaki, Tomigoro. Meiji 18 [1885], C. V. Starr East Asian Library, University of California, Berkeley.[14]

murder that involved choosing crime scene locations partially based on using a compass rose, and (d) he modified his compass rose by reducing the circular divisions to twelve in order to match his namesake celestial zodiac. Furthermore, the killer made multiple references to Japan, which turns out to be the one country in the world known for using a compass rose based on twelve equal divisions, a choice inspired by the zodiac — albeit the Chinese zodiac.

Can we say for certain that the killer knew about the Japanese practice of commingling the compass rose and the Chinese zodiac? Of course not. It's possible that the killer crafted his persona and conceived of his methodology without ever having learned about this historical curiosity. But then again, it's also possible that the killer did know about the practice and it inspired him to craft his methodology around the idea of dividing the nautical compass rose into twelve segments derived from the Western zodiac.

As with so many other aspects of this case, we'll likely never have a satisfactory answer. Nevertheless, it remains a compelling possibility.

4.2.2   The Codebreakers

The man we know as the Zodiac underwent an interesting evolution between October 1966 and August 1969. In particular, he began communicating with the Riverside Police Department and the *Press–Enterprise* through the taunting, but otherwise straightforward, letter known as "The Confession." A short while later, when he began writing to authorities and the press in the Bay Area, he added an unusual element to his communications, namely cryptography.

What could have motivated the killer to add this unique and bizarre dimension to his writing? Perhaps he had a lifelong fascination with cryptography. Perhaps the idea was simply born out of thinking about ways to make law enforcement look bad. These suggestions are both reasonable possibilities. But if we scrutinize events that took place between 1966 and 1969, we find yet another curiosity. Specifically, David Kahn's *The Codebreakers* — perhaps the best-known book ever written about cryptography — was published in 1967.

Many people who are knowledgeable about the Zodiac case are familiar with Kahn's book. Robert Graysmith mentioned it in his two books about the killer, and other researchers occasionally cite it as well. David Fincher went so far as to work a copy of the book into one of the scenes in *Zodiac*.

It's easy to imagine the killer learning of the book or possibly even reading it and being inspired to use cryptography in his next round of taunting communiqués. Interestingly, *The Codebreakers* says little that is directly applicable to the case of the Zodiac. In fact, the

Zodiac's actions directly contradict one of the few assertions Kahn makes in the book about criminals and their use of cryptography. In particular, on page 817 of the book, the author explains:

> *Criminals, like anyone else, will bother with codes and ciphers only when they have to, and the only time they really need them is in international smuggling, when illegal movements have to be coordinated in secrecy over great distances.*[15]

Of course, the Zodiac neither required the use of cipher out of any practical need for secrecy, nor did he use his ciphers as part of an international smuggling activity. Rather, the ciphers apparently satisfied a psychological need to taunt and torment both law enforcement and the public — a very real, albeit impractical, possibility that Kahn did not anticipate.

4.3 Noninfluences

Identifying concepts that the Zodiac may have used while constructing his murderous persona can provide insight into the thought processes of the man; however, it's also important to identify possible sources of inspiration that are unlikely to have played a role in the killer's formation of his alter ego. Dismissing these ideas is a valuable step forward because they represent analytical distractions that threaten to siphon our time and effort away from the elements of the case that truly deserve our attention.

4.3.1 Zodiac Watch Company

Another potential source of inspiration for the self-assigned name of the killer is the Zodiac watch company. This idea has been championed by Robert Graysmith largely owing to his primary suspect, Arthur Leigh Allen, having received such a watch as a gift sometime between Christmas of 1967 and the summer of 1969. The watch often strikes people as important not only because of the company's name but also because of the accompanying logo, a concentric cross and circle, which resembles the symbol the killer used to identify himself.

Graysmith has invested much into the perceived value of Allen's watch. In the introduction to *Zodiac Unmasked*, he declares: "But it had all begun with a watch."[3] Elsewhere he repeatedly makes the argument that the watch company is the only context in which the name "Zodiac" and the corresponding Zodiac symbol — the concentric cross and circle — appear together outside of the Zodiac case evidence.

In truth, the name and symbol do appear together in at least one other context. As pointed out by case expert Jake Wark and Graysmith himself in *Zodiac Unmasked*, there was a European model of car named Zodiac that had a hood ornament with a concentric cross and circle, similar to the Zodiac symbol.

Is the existence of the Zodiac watch company surprising? Is it meaningful? Many people think so, but I suggest otherwise. What we probably have at work here is something known as a joint-effect logical fallacy. This happens when causation is wrongfully asserted to exist between two events that are merely correlated owing to an underlying common cause. In our case, we have the word "zodiac" and the zodiac symbol appearing together in two different situations, not because one caused the other, but rather because the word and the symbol naturally go together. Specifically, the zodiac as a concept is symbolized by a circle graduated into twelve equal divisions. Moreover, when people represent information via a circle divided into twelve equal parts, it's common to abbreviate the representation with a circle divided into four equal parts. Doing so makes sense because the task of accurately showing all twelve divisions is often difficult. Furthermore, depending on the size of the circle and the circumstances of its existence, people may find the full representation overly crowded and challenging to interpret. Four divisions is a logical subset that is considerably easier to create and often easier to perceive. Familiar examples of this abbreviation include clock faces where the shown numbers have been reduced to 3, 6, 9, and 12.

When the killer decided to call himself the Zodiac and set out to create a symbol that represented this moniker, he probably chose the concentric cross and circle because it represented a subset of the full zodiac and could easily be drawn. In the case of the killer, there also probably was some duality at work in that the symbol could be thought of as representing the four quadrants of the killer's methodology. Similarly, when the Zodiac watch company set out to create a logo for itself, the people involved probably arrived at the same symbol based on similar considerations. In fact, for a watch company the symbol is even more appropriate precisely because clock faces are commonly abbreviated in an equivalent way. A similar type of evolution probably existed with the Zodiac vehicle and its corresponding hood ornament.

Twelve enjoys a special status as a number in that it's the first value that can be evenly divided by 1, 2, 3, and 4 — it is, of course, the product of 3 and 4. Also, it's divisible by 6 meaning that it's divisible by all numbers 1 through 6, except for 5. Therefore, when people create concepts that need to be easily divided into subsections — such as halves, thirds, quarters — the creation of twelve equal parts is a logical and highly functional choice. These considerations were undoubtedly in play when the nighttime sky was first divided into the signs of the zodiac more than 2,000 years ago. They also undoubtedly factored into people choosing to carve up the day into two sequences of twelve hours each.

With their similar representations of data — the zodiac dividing the nighttime sky into twelve equal sections and timepieces dividing the halves of the day into twelve equal hours — the two concepts have been naturally commingled for centuries. One of the most well-known instances of this phenomenon — other than the Zodiac watch company — is the historic St. Mark's Clock Tower in Venice, Italy, built circa 1500. This public timepiece has a prominent zodiac theme.

In the end, the Zodiac watch company is a curiosity. There is no compelling evidence that the killer was inspired by it. Moreover, the idea of the killer being inspired by a watch feels shallow. Naming oneself after a watch appears to make as much sense as naming oneself after any other inanimate object. And to be precise, the watch company is named Zodiac; as previously emphasized, the killer called himself *the* Zodiac. This subtle difference — that notably was never appreciated by Graysmith — is an important point that provides more evidence that the watch company was not the source of the self-assigned name.

In contrast, we can infer that the killer possessed considerable knowledge about the celestial zodiac and that he used this knowledge to craft a persona and build a methodology. The concept of the zodiac clearly was a primary inspiration to the killer.

4.3.2   Radian Angle

When the Zodiac wrote the following postscript to the *Mikado* Letter — probably in response to Paul Avery's simplistic and flawed analysis of the Phillips 66 map — he provided the case evidence with a much-discussed and controversial tidbit.

PS. The Mt. Diablo Code concerns
Radians + # inches along the radians

4.3.2.1   What Are Radians?

A radian is a unit of angular measure, similar in purpose to the more common degree. There are 360° in a circle; the equivalent value in radians is 2π. Given that $\pi = 3.14159\ldots$, 2π translates into approximately 6.28 radians.

Upon first consideration, this way of measuring angles seems strange and unnatural. However, the point to understand with radians is that the unit was not conceived from an isolated desire to create a new unit for measuring angles but rather out of mathematical convenience. In other words, by measuring angles in this way, other mathematical manipulations involving those angles often become more straightforward. In this sense, the unit was more discovered than it was created, and, hence, its characteristics have little to do with satisfying human intuition.

4.3.2.2 The Radian Theory

One of the reasons that the radian postscript is so infamous is because of a particular theory that it spawned. In the late 1980s, a man named Gareth Penn self-published a book entitled *Times 17*.[16] In my view, this book is filled with wild speculation, most of which is almost certainly incorrect. It also openly accused a man of being the Zodiac — a man who is, quite clearly, innocent. Yet one of Penn's lines of speculation, an idea that has come to be known as the Radian Theory, resonated with many people who were intrigued by the case. Later, the popularity of the theory was bolstered when Penn appeared in the 1999 documentary *Case Reopened*.[2]

The essence of the theory is that the Zodiac chose Blue Rock Springs and Presidio Heights as crime scenes because they form an angle — with the vertex being Mount Diablo — of approximately one radian. The genesis of this idea came about at a time when some of the exact wording of the Zodiac's letters had not been released to the public. In particular, Penn learned of the reference to radians from his father who had read some of the letters as an employee of the California Attorney General's office.[17] Because of some misquoting, however, Penn thought the content referred to "a radian" or "a radian angle," which he interpreted to mean an angle measuring exactly one radian — about 57.3°. Later, once Penn learned of the precise wording used in the relevant parts of the Zodiac letters, the subtle but important differences were not enough to change his mind about the theory. This reluctance to reconsider his position is, perhaps, understandable given that Penn described the discovery of the "radian angle" as " ... the most shocking experience of my entire life."[17]

I contend that Penn was partially correct in that the angle he identified was (a) intentionally constructed by the Zodiac and (b) an important part of the killer's methodology. But, in terms of the other aspects of his theory, I believe Penn was incorrect. In particular, as noted regarding the killer's use of the compass rose, the Zodiac constructed the angle in question as an approximation of 60°, not an exact radian. Furthermore, to discover the relevant angles, one need only follow the instructions provided by the killer himself—set the annotated Zodiac symbol to magnetic north. No inference based on radians or anything similar is required. In my view, the radian theory is little more than an unfortunate by-product of the coincidence that one radian is nearly 60°.

4.3.2.3 All For Naught?

What then are we to make of the Zodiac's use of the term "radians"? Was the killer simply accustomed to using the unit? Was he going out of his way to come across as an intelligent and educated person? Possibly. But there is another subtler possibility.

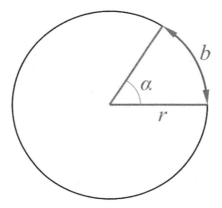

Figure 4.3: The geometric definition of a radian. A one-radian angle is formed when the shown distance along the circumference of a circle is equal to the radius, in other words, $r = b$. Credit: This image is in the public domain.*

When the mathematical specifics of this concept were being finalized circa 1875, the people who named the unit a radian did so partially because it can be considered a contraction of the phrase "radial angle."[18] This meaning is also evident in the precise definition of a radian, shown in Figure 4.3. Specifically, on a given circle, a one-radian

---

* *http://zodiacrevisited.com/book/radian-image*

angle is formed between two radii when the corresponding section of the circumference is the same length as the radius. This perspective illustrates why a radian is a "radial angle"; the angle is defined in terms of radial lines, in other words, lines that project outward from the center of a circle.

Since the Zodiac was referring to angles formed by radial lines — specifically the 30° lines extending outward from the center of the rotated compass rose — it's easy to imagine that he may have chosen to use the word "radians" precisely because the unit is defined in terms of a scenario that is similar to the one he was trying to describe. In fact, the term can even be thought of as a clue suggesting how to properly interpret the modified compass rose, in other words, pay attention to the angles formed by the described radial lines.

If true, this possibility suggests that the killer had significant knowledge of mathematics. As a computer engineer, I have achieved some level of accomplishment in the study of mathematics. Although I don't claim to be an exceptional mathematician, my understanding of the subject is well above average. Yet even with a solid understanding of mathematics, it took me many years of Zodiac research to appreciate this subtle interpretation of radians and how the unit applies to the subject matter. Therefore, if the killer did choose this unit based on these considerations, I have to believe that the man had some appreciable level of formal education in either mathematics, engineering, or the physical sciences.

4.4 Conclusion

Although we may not be able to say for sure whether the influences discussed in this chapter played a role in the creation of the Zodiac persona, or to what degree, we can make one statement with certainty: the killer's construction of the persona was a substantial undertaking that clearly required considerable time, effort, and thought. The man did not just haphazardly choose to call himself the Zodiac one morning after flipping through the newspaper and seeing the horoscope section. It is much more likely that he showed up in San Francisco with the idea of crafting a sophisticated, multilayered, public persona that would embody the characteristics that he valued. He probably worked at creating the persona in much the same way that organizations labor over every word of a mission statement. By the time the killer settled on the Zodiac, with its related methodology, underlying meaning, and symbolism, the result was a work of art in his mind. It was his masterpiece — a personal, albeit anonymous, representation of himself. It was a statement about who he was and what he was doing, the dark product of a creative endeavor in which the killer took great pride.

Notes

1. Robert Graysmith, *Zodiac*, New York: Berkley Books, 1987.

2. MacCarthy, P. K., director, *Case Reopened*, Season 1, Episode 1, *The Zodiac*, October 10, 1999.

3. Robert Graysmith, *Zodiac Unmasked: The Identity of America's Most Elusive Serial Killer Revealed*, New York: Berkley Books, 2002.

4. Irving Pichel and Ernest B. Schoedsack, directors, *The Most Dangerous Game*, RKO Studios, 1932.

5. Malcolm Glover, "Hundreds of 'Zodiac' Tips Flood Bay Police," *San Francisco Examiner*, October 18, 1969, 1.

6. "Police Plan Strategy to Trap Zodiac," *San Francisco Examiner*, October 21, 1969, 1.

7. Norman Foster, director, *Charlie Chan at Treasure Island*, 20th Century Fox, 1939.

8. Paul Avery, "Gilbert and Sullivan Clue to Zodiac," *San Francisco Chronicle*, October 12, 1970, 5.

9. Ian Bradley, *The Complete Annotated Gilbert & Sullivan*, New York: Oxford University Press, 1996, p. 572.

10. *The Bell Telephone Hour, The Mikado*, LP recording: OL-5480, Columbia Masterworks, 1960.

11. Bob Varney, *Gilbert & Sullivan: The Mikado*, audio digitization, October 13, 2010, Accessed November 25, 2020, *http://zodiacrevisited.com/book/mikdado-lp-1960-online*.

12. Norman Campbell and Martyn Green, directors, *The Bell Telephone Hour*, Season 2, Episode 13, April 29, 1960.

13. Helen Wallis and Arthur Howard Robinson, *Cartographical Innovations: An International Handbook of Mapping Terms to 1900*, London: Map Collector Publications Ltd, 1987.

14. Tomigoro Ozaki, *Hanken Menkyo Doban Yokohama Chizu*, C. V. Starr East Asian Library, University of California, Berkeley, 1885, Accessed November 25, 2020, *http://zodiacrevisited.com/book/ucb-yokohama-map*.

15. David Kahn, *The Codebreakers: The Story of Secret Writing*, New York: The Macmillan Company, 1967, p. 817.

16. Gareth Penn, *Times 17: The Amazing Story of the Zodiac Murders in California and Massachusetts, 1966-1981*, Foxglove Press, 1987.

17. Penn, *Times 17*, p. 3.

18. Jeff Miller, *Earliest Known Uses of Some of the Words of Mathematics (R)*, Accessed November 25, 2020, *http://zodiacrevisited.com/book/miller-radian*.

5

Understanding the Ciphers

We intend to begin on the first of February unrestricted submarine warfare....

Deciphered Zimmerman Telegram sent by the Germans that precipitated the United States' entry into World War I, January 1917

Interestingly, the Zodiac's four ciphers can be thought of as a microcosm of the larger Zodiac case. The 408 — the only cipher that, thus far, has an accepted solution — provides us with real and meaningful clues about the killer. We can think of this cryptogram as representing the plentiful yet ultimately unsatisfactory set of facts that we do know about the case.

At the other end of the spectrum is the 340 cipher. Analysis suggests that this cipher should be solvable. Although many people have *claimed* to have solved the 340, nobody has presented a convincing solution.* In other words, these people truly believe their solutions,

---

*After more than five decades, the Zodiac's 340 cipher was finally solved in December 2020. See Section 5.3.5 for more details.

however, the claims do not withstand the test of scrutiny. In this sense, solving the 340 is akin to identifying the killer and solving the case of the Zodiac. People continually convince themselves that they've solved the case, but most cannot convince anybody else, and no solution has been universally accepted.

Finally, the two remaining ciphers are so short that they may never be solved to the satisfaction of most people. Putting aside the fact that I'm proposing solutions for these ciphers, someone could come forward tomorrow with the correct solutions, and, undoubtedly, there would be many people who would argue against them. The best hope we have for arriving at undisputed solutions to these cryptograms is identifying the killer while he's still alive and having him explain them to us. Of course, that scenario is unlikely. As such, these ciphers symbolize the minutiae in the case that, similarly, we may never fully understand. For example, did the killer actually believe his victims would become his slaves in the afterlife? Did he really intend to blow up a school bus? And, of course, the more overt question: exactly which murders did the killer commit? Cheri Jo Bates? Robert Domingos and Linda Edwards? How about the murders less commonly attributed to him, such as Richard Radetich and Joyce and Johnny Ray Swindle?

These parallels between the ciphers and the larger case of the Zodiac make the cryptograms that much more interesting and, in some sense, that much more frustrating. They are literally a mystery within a mystery.

There is also an argument to be made that the ciphers are the best remaining opportunity for the world to identify the killer — recent advancements in the forensic use of DNA notwithstanding, perhaps. The killer's courting of Melvin Belli — a nationally renowned defense attorney — by way of the Belli Letter and his other possible actions may have been rooted in an expectation of impending apprehension. One reason he may have anticipated being caught is that he knew the solution to the 340 contained some information that, once revealed, would quite likely allow law enforcement to identify him. Perhaps he nervously waited for an eventuality that never came to pass.

Less speculatively, perhaps one day the solution to the "My Name Is" cipher actually will provide us with the killer's name. While many facts in the Zodiac case have been understood for several decades, the unsolved ciphers are some of the few dormant seeds that may yet, one day, bear the fruit of newfound information.

In this chapter, I briefly review some basic background knowledge required for discussing the ciphers. I then analyze each of the four Zodiac ciphers, reviewing what's known and what we can reasonably conclude from the knowledge. Along the way, I offer probable solutions to the two shorter ciphers. Although these solutions cannot be completely validated given the state of the evidence, I explain why I feel there is a high probability that they are, indeed, correct. Finally, I discuss some modern efforts that have been and continue to be undertaken in the hopes of solving the 340.

5.1   Background

When considering the case of the Zodiac, many people shy away from the ciphers because of a perception that the topic requires some esoteric expertise or a mathematical background. Honestly, there's no need for this hesitance. Armed with a little knowledge, anyone can understand the ciphers. In this section, I review the requisite background. Most of it's straightforward. The only exception I will concede regards polyalphabetic ciphers, which are discussed in Section 5.1.5 and can be confusing. If it's not making sense, skip it. The topic, while valuable in terms of providing some context for the killer's choice of cipher, is not an essential part of understanding the Zodiac's use of cryptography.

5.1.1   Terminology

Unavoidably, discussions of ciphers involve some specialized terms. To pave the way for the discussion that follows, I define some relevant terms here.

plaintext: A message as it reads before encipherment, or alternatively, after correct decipherment.

ciphertext: An enciphered message. All the ciphers written by the Zodiac are in the form of ciphertext.

symbol: A letter, number, or other type of character used to represent a part of the plaintext. While other approaches are possible, the common approach — and the approach we will focus on for the purposes of this chapter — is to have one symbol represent one plaintext letter. The Zodiac's 408 cipher uses fifty-four different symbols including, letters, numbers, backward letters, and various geometric shapes. Each one corresponds to a single letter of the alphabet.

symbol instance: A particular instance of a single symbol in the ciphertext representing a single letter from the plaintext. The killer's 408 cipher has fifty-four unique symbols, but 408 symbol instances (hence the name). While others may use this term occasionally, it's not a commonly accepted cryptography term such as "plaintext" and "ciphertext." Nevertheless, I find it valuable to explicitly define the term so it's meaning is clear in the following descriptions.

By convention, ciphertext is shown in **UPPERCASE** and plaintext in **lowercase**. To illustrate these definitions and the convention, consider the encipherment of the word "example" shown in Figure 5.1.

```
Plaintext   e  x  a  m  p  l  e
Ciphertext  H  A  D  P  S  O  H
```

Figure 5.1: Enciphering the word "example"

The plaintext is just the word itself. For the ciphertext, each letter of the plaintext has been replaced with a different letter. In this case, the symbols are simply letters of our alphabet, just different letters than the ones they actually represent. The cipher has a total of seven symbol instances, one for each occurrence of each letter in the word. However, there are only six symbols, since the symbol **H** (corresponding to plaintext letter **e**) occurs twice.

As a matter of convenience, when the meaning is clear, I will sometimes use the word symbols to describe what are technically symbol instances. This choice is a bit of imprecision that allows us to avoid tedious and unhelpful repetition.

5.1.2 Cryptography

Cryptography is the science and practice of secret communication. Countless societies have employed various forms of cryptography over the last two-plus millennia. For the vast majority of that time, cryptography mostly supported sensitive military communications and other government-related activities requiring secrecy. But with the advent of the computer revolution, cryptography has evolved into a particularly important part of computer-network communications, one that plays a critical role in enabling the secure transmission of sensitive information all over the world. Due to the magnitude of this turning point, people often divide cryptography into two eras: the precomputer era and the modern or contemporary era. When referring to the precomputer era, the subject is often referred to as classical cryptography.

Within classical cryptography, there are several notable subdivisions. The most important distinction concerns codes and ciphers. Many people think that all forms of secret writing are codes. To be technically precise, a code involves the substitution of words or phrases. And since there is no systematic way to apply such substitutions, people encoding and decoding a given code must share a common codebook that documents the numerous translations.

Ciphers, on the other hand, involve substitution at a subword level. Typically, ciphers will map one letter to a different letter or symbol. Some ciphers, however, work on groups of letters rather than individual letters. In a practical sense, ciphers are often superior to codes in that the knowledge required to encipher or decipher a message is relatively little. Instead of using a codebook that might have thousands of word mappings, the user of a cipher need only know a small number of letter mappings. Furthermore, this information is often simplified such that the user only has to remember a few specifics of a cipher algorithm — the particular process through which one maps plaintext to ciphertext — and a keyword used to guide the application of said algorithm.[*]

5.1.3 Simple Substitution Ciphers

The simplest form of a cipher is something called, appropriately enough, a simple substitution cipher. For this type of cipher, a unique symbol — often a different letter of the same alphabet — replaces each letter of the alphabet. Julius Caesar famously used a cipher of this sort that involved shifting the letters of the alphabet by three positions, with any letters falling off the end wrapping around to the beginning. For this reason, ciphers constructed by any simple position shift are often called Caesar shift ciphers or sometimes just Caesar ciphers. The example from Figure 5.1 is a standard three-position Caesar shift cipher, as is the first mapping shown in Figure 5.2.

Cryptographers also construct simple substitution ciphers that are not Caesar shift ciphers. For example, if we randomly map letters in the alphabet to other letters in the same alphabet, instead of systematically shifting them, we still have a simple substitution cipher — each letter is substituted with a different, single, unique letter — but, it would not be a Caesar shift cipher. Similarly, there is no requirement that we limit our symbols to letters in our simple substitution cipher. We could, just as well, replace all the letters in our alphabet with numbers or, for that matter, any arbitrary set of symbols. Figure 5.2 shows examples of such mappings.

---

[*]Because of the circumstances surrounding the Zodiac's use of ciphers, keywords are not a factor, so I will not cover them.

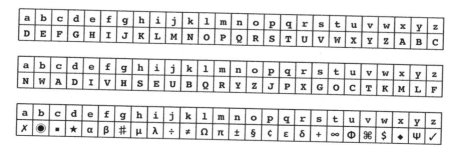

Figure 5.2: Three examples of simple substitution mappings. In each case, the first row is the plaintext alphabet and the second row shows the corresponding ciphertext symbols. The first example is a standard three-position Caesar shift cipher — **a** maps to **D**, **b** to **E**, and so on. The second example continues to use letters as symbols, but the mapping is random instead of a Caesar shift. The final example illustrates the use of arbitrary, nonalphabetic symbols instead of letters.

5.1.4   Cryptanalysis

For just as long as people have been constructing secret messages, other people have been attempting to deconstruct them without knowing the particulars of the encryption process. This task is known as cryptanalysis.

The most valuable benefit of a simple substitution cipher is that it is, indeed, simple. Both enciphering and deciphering are easy. When cryptanalysis was in its infancy, simple substitution ciphers provided an adequate degree of secrecy. But as practitioners in the art of cryptanalysis made early advances, simple substitution ciphers quickly became unacceptably insecure.

The particular characteristic of simple substitution ciphers that cryptanalysts exploited in order to extract a solution is the fact that not all letters are created equally. For example, some letters often appear together while others effectively never do. The sequence **th** is highly probable. On the other hand, the sequence **qx** is a practical impossibility. But, when considering simple substitution ciphers, the single-most useful differentiator between individual letters is a simple measure of how often the letter occurs, on average, in standard text. For example, the English language has at its extremes the letters **e** and **z**. For a given piece of English text that consists of 1,000 letters, statistics suggest we should expect **e** to occur approximately 127 times, whereas **z** might occur once, if at all. Since a symbol from a simple substitution cipher occurs the same number of times as the plaintext letter that it conceals, this characteristic provides a significant analytical foothold from which a skilled cryptanalyst can extract a solution.

As an example, consider a simple substitution cipher with a length of 1,000 characters and a symbol occurrence breakdown as shown in Figure 5.3. Because the ciphertext symbol **I** occurs 129 times, we can say with near certainty that **I** does not represent the letter **z**. Furthermore, it's an excellent candidate for the plaintext letter **e**, which we expect to occur about 127 times given the length of the cipher. This particular cryptanalytic technique is known as frequency analysis. The first known description of the technique dates back to a scholarly Arab treatise from the ninth century.[1] The evolution of cryptanalysis progressed more slowly in Europe, but by the 1500s, practitioners of the art of cipher breaking were using frequency analysis on a regular basis.

Certainly, the statistical characteristics of a given piece of plaintext may well stray from the profile that represents so-called standard text. As an extreme and interesting example, an author named Ernest Vincent Wright wrote a 1939 novel entitled *Gadsby*. This work secured its place in literary history by virtue of not having a single letter **e** in any of its 50,000 words. As such, it remains one of the most ambitious examples of a linguistic art form known as constrained writing. Although enciphered text is unlikely to be as contrived as the prose of *Gadsby*, the book, nevertheless, illustrates that meaningful content may well deviate from the norm, and possibly substantially so. More relevant to our particular interest is the related observation that the shorter the cipher, the more likely it is to deviate from the characteristics of standard text, since unintentional deviations usually average themselves out over time.

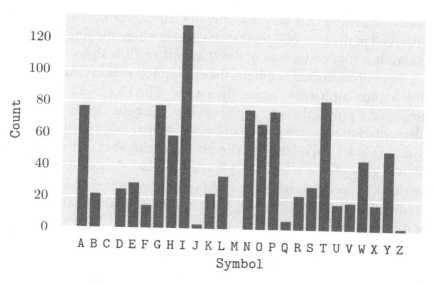

Figure 5.3: The frequency distribution of a simple substitution cipher created from the first 1,000 characters of Mary Shelley's classic novel *Frankenstein; or, The Modern Prometheus*. We can conclude that the symbol **I** is probably concealing the letter **e** since we should expect **e** to occur about 127 times and **I** occurs exactly 129 times. Unsurprisingly, **I** is, indeed, **e**.

Regardless of all these caveats related to letter frequency, the eventual conclusion is inescapable: it's effectively impossible to make a simple substitution cipher secure for meaningful messages of any significant length.

In order to combat frequency analysis, cryptographers began to devise more sophisticated ciphers that not only concealed the enciphered message but also hid the frequencies of the underlying plaintext letters. Those efforts yielded two common approaches: polyalphabetic ciphers and homophonic substitution ciphers.

5.1.5   Polyalphabetic Ciphers

Because simple substitution ciphers always map plaintext letters to a single ciphertext equivalent, the ciphers are said to be monoalphabetic — meaning that they use only one alphabet. This idea is easily observed in the case of Caesar shift ciphers where the single alphabet is simply a rotated version of the standard English alphabet.

For polyalphabetic ciphers, the encryption process involves multiple cipher alphabets, hence the name. The most well-known example of a polyalphabetic cipher is the Vigenère cipher whose implementation requires a table of cipher alphabets. Specifically, there is one row for each letter in the plaintext alphabet. In each incremental row of the table, the plaintext alphabet is shifted — in the sense of a Caesar cipher — one additional position. For English, the resultant table has twenty-six Caesar shift cipher alphabets spread across twenty-six rows. An example of a Vigenère table is shown in Figure 5.4.

In order to implement the Vigenère algorithm, each time a given plaintext letter is enciphered, the cipher alphabet changes to a different alphabet, or row, in the table. Usually, the decision of which row to use is determined by way of a keyword. As a consequence, a given plaintext letter could be mapped to any letter in the plaintext alphabet, including possibly itself. What matters is the current state of the table sequencing when the time comes for the plaintext letter to be enciphered.

The Vigenère cipher in particular and polyalphabetic ciphers in general represented a significant advancement in the cryptographic strength of ciphers. Cryptanalytic techniques to attack polyalphabetic ciphers required considerably more sophisticated statistical analysis.

But polyalphabetic ciphers are not perfect; they have their own set of issues, not the least of which is their complexity. Under some circumstances, cryptographers desired a compromise approach — something that improved the cryptographic strength of simple substitution ciphers but avoided the complications of polyalphabetic ciphers. A class of ciphers known as monoalphabetic with complexities provided that compromise. Perhaps the most common type of cipher from this class is the homophonic substitution cipher.

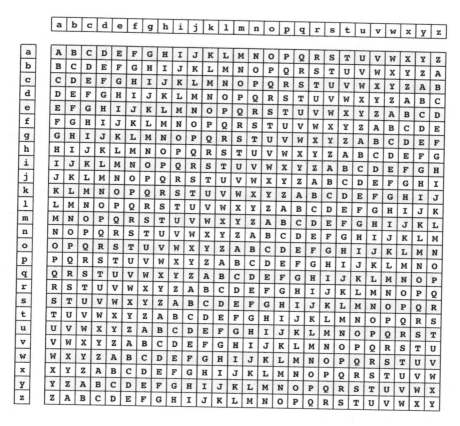

Figure 5.4: A Vigenère table. Each plaintext letter can be mapped to any one of twenty-six different Caesar shift alphabets.

5.1.6 Homophonic Substitution Ciphers

As previously stated, the weakness of a simple substitution cipher comes from the frequency characteristics of the plaintext letters being evident in the symbols of the ciphertext. In particular, the high-frequency ciphertext symbols are, quite likely, a telltale sign of high-frequency plaintext letters.

Homophonic substitution ciphers aim to fix this deficiency by adding more ciphertext symbols. Plaintext letters that are used often are enciphered with multiple ciphertext symbols. The more often a given plaintext letter is used, the more ciphertext symbols are used to encipher the letter. When compared to a simple substitution cipher, the ciphertext of a homophonic substitution cipher will have more symbols and the frequency of the symbols will be more nearly uniform. For example, if you find a given ciphertext symbol has a frequency of 2 percent, you would not know if it's a low-frequency letter such as **c**, or if it's one of several symbols that are being used to encipher a high-frequency letter such as **e**.

Through this description, we can see the meaning of the term "homophonic." Of course, "homo" means same, and "phonic" means sound. In other words, the cipher is constructed using ciphertext symbols that have the same sound, which is a way — albeit a slightly strange way — of saying that they map to the same plaintext letter. Relatedly, people use the word "homophones" to describe the set of equivalent symbols that are used to encipher a given letter. For example, we should expect a high-frequency letter, such as **e**, to have several homophones.

It's important to understand the relationship between plaintext letters and ciphertext symbols. Specifically, a given letter may have multiple ciphertext symbols. Although there are no strict rules in terms of the number of ciphertext symbols that must be used for a given letter, the value of homophonic substitution requires that generally, the higher the frequency of the plaintext letter, the larger the number of ciphertext symbols that should be used. Equally important is the other direction of the relationship. For a homophonic substitution cipher, a given ciphertext symbol will map to one and only one letter.

Herein lies an important distinction between polyalphabetic ciphers and homophonic substitution ciphers. For the polyalphabetic ciphers, a given ciphertext symbol will correspond to multiple plaintext letters because each ciphertext symbol belongs to multiple alphabets, and each alphabet maps the symbol to a different plaintext letter. On the other hand, for a homophonic substitution cipher, any ciphertext symbol corresponds to a single plaintext letter; there are just more symbols compared with a simple substitution cipher. These relationships are shown in Figure 5.5.

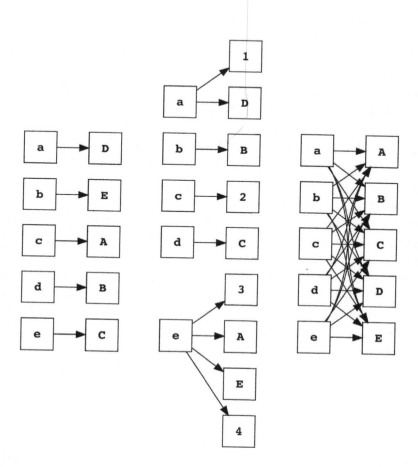

Figure 5.5: Example letter-to-symbol mappings for three different types of ciphers. To limit complexity, the alphabet has been reduced to **a–e**. On the left is a Caesar cipher. The plaintext letters are simply mapped to other letters in the same alphabet. The middle mapping is a homophonic substitution cipher. High frequency plaintext letters receive additional ciphertext symbols in order to hide their frequency characteristics. The letters of the alphabet can be used for the ciphertext symbols, but more symbols are required. In this case, numbers have been used for the additional symbols. The right mapping is a polyalphabetic cipher. The cipher symbols are again the letters of the plaintext alphabet. This time, however, any plaintext letter can map to any ciphertext symbol — the precise mapping changes each time a letter is enciphered.

5.2   The Zodiac's Ciphers

The Zodiac is known to have created four ciphers. For ease of reference, these ciphers are referred to based on the number of symbol instances in each cipher: 408, 340, 13, and 32. The 13 cipher is often called the "My Name Is" cipher based on the letter in which it appeared and its supposed message. To date, the 408 is the only one of the four that has been solved. Through its solution, the cipher was definitively shown to be a homophonic substitution cipher. The remaining ciphers, though unsolved, appear to be similar to the 408 in many respects and therefore are, quite likely, also homophonic substitution ciphers. The only caveat applies to the 340, which analysis suggests may involve some additional forms of complexity. From a practical perspective, the 340 cipher is probably solvable if someone can gain enough insight into the particulars of these additional complexities. In contrast, the "My Name Is" cipher and the 32 cipher are so short and involve so few repeated symbols that they probably will not be solved — at least not verifiably — without the benefit of context knowledge such as additional supporting information from the case or an explanation from the man who created them. Nevertheless, I will propose probable solutions for both of these ciphers.

5.2.1   Choice of Symbols

One consequence of the way in which homophonic substitution works is that it requires significantly more symbols than the number of letters in the plaintext alphabet that it enciphers. For example, the Zodiac's 408 cipher used fifty-four symbols to encipher twenty-three of the twenty-six letters in our alphabet — the letters **j**, **q**, and **z** were not used in the plaintext. Of course, the letters of the alphabet themselves are available for use as ciphertext symbols, each presumably corresponding to a different plaintext letter. However, many other symbols will be required. Because of these constraints, people using homophonic substitution ciphers will often forgo using letters and other symbols altogether and, instead, will resort to using numbers. As we know, the Zodiac chose to use symbols, including letters, backward letters, a variety of constructions based on simple geometric shapes, and a handful of other symbols.

Much has been made of the particular symbols that the Zodiac used in his four ciphers. People sometimes claim that many of the symbols correspond to one particular alphabet or another. Others claim that some of the symbols indicate knowledge of a specific field of study such as semaphore which is often used by navies. In my estimation, too much has been made of these possibilities. The killer simply needed more symbols than the alphabet itself provided. The symbols are all basic in structure. It's completely within the realm of possibility that he thought up these symbols as he needed them. Certainly, the man may have used some of the symbols based on his familiarity with them through prior experience. But whether he did is effectively unknowable, and it's just as likely that he did not.

5.2.2   The 408 Cipher

The 408 is the cipher with which the killer announced his existence. One-third of the cipher accompanied each of the three letters that the killer simultaneously sent to three Bay Area newspapers: the *Chronicle*, the *Examiner*, and the *Vallejo Times-Herald*. All three letters were postmarked July 31, 1969. Naval cryptanalysts tried to solve the cipher but were unable to do so before Donald and Bettye Harden, a Salinas high school teacher and his wife, cracked it. The solution, documented in Section 2.6 of *The Zodiac Revisited, Volume 1*, revealed a disturbing celebration of murder.

As the only cipher to have been definitively solved,* the 408 is a source of much insight into the killer's use of cryptography. First and foremost, the cryptogram is a straightforward version of a homophonic substitution cipher. With the exception of a few cases where the killer made simple mistakes, perhaps intentionally, each symbol

---

*The 340 cipher was finally solved near the time of this book's publication. See *http://zodiacrevisited.com/book/340-solution* for more information.

corresponds to exactly one letter. Also, per standard cipher construction practices, neither spaces nor punctuation were included.

As the name implies, the cipher consists of 408 symbol instances. The killer's message began with the first symbol and continued through instance 390. In other words, there were an extra eighteen symbols at the end of the cipher. Of course, when the cipher was mailed, there was no indication as to the order of the three different sections. Since the killer had arranged each section into identical layouts of 136 symbol instances arranged in eight rows and seventeen columns, any of the sections could have been in position one, two, or three. Part of solving the cipher required determining the proper order of the three sections.

Many have speculated that the final eighteen symbols, which decipher to **ebeorietemethhpiti**, may represent a signature or somehow provide other clues to the identity of the author. People who have made this suggestion include one of the original Vallejo detectives assigned to the case and Dr. D. C. B. Marsh, the man who originally validated the Hardens' solution.[2] In fact, Donald Harden himself acknowledged the possibility and explained that he and his wife had spent time trying to further decipher the last line;[3] however, soon after, he publicly proclaimed that the eighteen symbols were probably just "filler."[4]

One of the suggestions that received some attention in the days following the publication of the Hardens' solution was that the deciphered eighteen symbols were an anagram of: "Robert Emmet the hippie."[5] This possibility is simply not correct. Beyond the questionable reliance on anagramming, the proposal is also plagued by the fact that the plaintext is missing an instance of each **m**, **p**, and **r**; also, there is an extra **i**.

By far, the most probable explanation for these eighteen symbols is that they are indeed filler symbols that the killer added to complete the final section of the 408. If he had chosen to simply stop the cipher at the end of the content — in other words, create a 390 character cipher instead of a 408 character cipher — the final section would have had fewer symbol instances than the other two sections, which would have made it obvious that the shorter section belonged in the last position. Additionally, stopping the content right at the end of the cipher would have provided another clue in that one could assume that the last symbol instance was an end-of-word boundary. By having additional filler symbols, the positioning of the final word is hidden.

One of the fascinating aspects of the Zodiac case is that people continue to make valuable discoveries hidden in the evidence, even decades after the initial publication or release of the information. Brax Sisco, the original creator of the computer program *zkdecrypto*, discussed in Section 5.3.3, made one such discovery in 2009 when he pointed out that an unexpectedly large number of the symbols used for the final seventeen characters (the last row) appear elsewhere in their respective columns.[6] In fact, this characteristic of the final row is so unlike all other rows in the cipher that it's highly unlikely to have come about as a matter of mere coincidence. Furthermore, this peculiarity is not only compelling evidence of the last line being simple filler but also of the process by which the killer chose the symbols; namely, he took an existing symbol at random from elsewhere in the column. Some people describe this process as "pulling down" a random symbol. This was an important observation that nobody had made in forty years of looking at the 408 cipher. As a corollary to the observation, any attempt at finding meaning in these last eighteen symbols is almost certainly a waste of time.

*   *   *

I believe the killer carefully constructed the content of the 408 cipher intending its length to be somewhere between 391 and 408 characters; in other words, to have it end somewhere in the final row of the cipher. However, he made a mistake. If we look at the transition from the second to the third section of the cipher, it's clear that the author accidentally omitted a word. Because of this omission, the number of filler symbols increased to eighteen instead of being some number less than seventeen.

The word that the killer omitted probably was **people**. With this word added, the sentence would read:

```
I WILL BE REBORN IN PARADICE AND ALL
THE PEOPLE I HAVE KILLED WILL BECOME
MY SLAVES
```

The transition from the second to the third section happens between the letters **h** and **e** in the word **the**. Notice how both **the** and **people** end in the letter **e**, which is the letter that begins the third section of the cipher. In all probability, the killer simply lost track of which word he was enciphering when he made the transition from section two to section three. Therefore, he probably intended to have twelve symbols left over at the end of the cipher not eighteen.

* * *

Another interesting aspect of the 408 concerns the way it was enciphered; specifically, the way the author assigned plaintext letters to ciphertext symbols. Since a homophonic substitution cipher has several letters represented by multiple symbols, a person creating such a cipher has many choices in terms of which symbol to use each time he or she needs to encipher a high-frequency letter. One way to handle this set of choices is to determine the number of symbols that will be used for each letter and systematically cycle through all available options, always using the same order. This approach is known as sequential assignment. The benefits of sequential assignment are twofold. First, the use of equivalent symbols is guaranteed to be evenly distributed across the available choices. In other words, you will not end up with one symbol used many times while another symbol for the same letter is used only a few times. Second, the encryption process is especially regular; at any given point, there is no uncertainty about which symbol to use next. Interestingly, there is also a disadvantage to sequential assignment. Specifically, the systematic selection of homophones can leave telltale clues in the ciphertext that an experienced cryptanalyst can exploit.[7] From a pure cipher strength perspective, it's best to choose the homophones through some type of random, unpredictable approach.

So, how did the Zodiac select homophones when creating the 408 cipher? Throughout most of the cipher, he used sequential assignment for several of the symbols. But toward the end of the cipher, he broke from sequential assignment and used a random approach. We can reach this conclusion by listing out the plaintext letters and, for each one, enumerating its respective homophones in the order that they appear in the cipher. I summarize the results of doing this in Table 5.1.

Category	Count
No Homophones (only one symbol)	11
Nonsequential	2
Perfectly Sequential	1
Initially Sequential	9

Table 5.1: A Breakdown of 408 plaintext letter encipherment by category

As you can see, there are nine letters that are initially sequential, meaning the killer started out using sequential assignment but later abandoned it. Although it's impossible to point to a specific location in the cipher and say that the killer abandoned sequential assignment from this position forward, an inspection of the data reveals that the change mostly happened in the latter third of the cipher.

This observation, together with the omission of a word when transitioning from section two to section three, suggests that the killer may have carefully created the first two-thirds of the cipher and then, for some reason, had an interruption in his work. When he returned, he may have hastily finished the cipher, losing track of the precise transition point — resulting in the omitted word — and possibly the state of his homophone sequencing. We know that the timing of the letters that accompanied the ciphers felt a bit unrealistic; they were postmarked July 31 and demanded publication by August 1. Perhaps, the killer was working to a self-imposed deadline that necessitated he finish the partially completed cipher faster, and, hence, less carefully, than he otherwise would have. Speculative thoughts, to be sure, but they do offer a reasonable explanation for these subtle characteristics found in the 408.

5.2.3   The 340 Cipher

The Zodiac's second known foray into the world of cipher crafting resulted in what is widely regarded as the most interesting of the killer's ciphers, the 340. In this case, the killer meticulously constructed the cipher and sent it along with the Dripping Pen Card, which he mailed November 8, 1969, near the height of his terroristic grip on the Bay Area.

In many respects, the 340 looks similar to the 408. Like its predecessor, it's comprised of a large number of symbols including letters, backward letters, and an eclectic mix of nonalphabetic symbols. Additionally, as shown in Figure 5.6, the killer again used a strict grid-like arrangement consisting of seventeen columns per row. Of course, a different message length resulted in a different number of rows — twenty in the case of the 340 versus twenty-four for the 408. As with the 408, the final row of the 340 contains a full set of seventeen symbol instances.

These characteristics suggest that the 340 is also a homophonic substitution cipher, at least fundamentally. Again, the end of the cipher probably contains filler symbols designed to frustrate decipherment. In fact, the last half of the last row includes six ciphertext symbols that unmistakably spell a modified version of the word **ZODIAC**. These are likely filler symbols that are serving a secondary purpose of being a signature.

Yet, the differences between the 408 and the 340 are also tellingly important. For a given straight homophonic substitution cipher, there are two principal ways in which the person creating the cipher can increase its cryptographic strength. The first is to reduce the cipher's length by reducing the length of the enciphered message. This approach decreases the amount of data that a would-be cipher

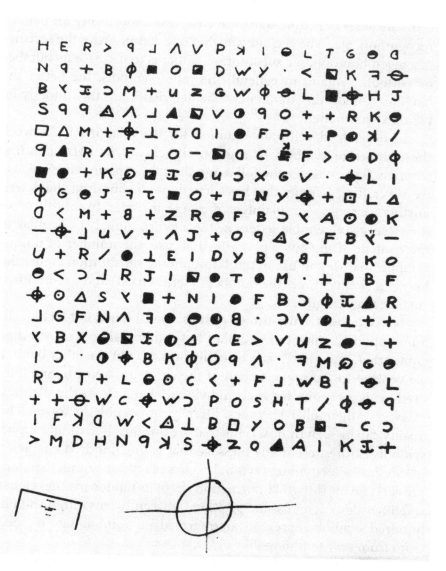

Figure 5.6: The Zodiac's 340 cipher that accompanied the Dripping Pen Card. Image reproduced with permission from the *San Francisco Chronicle* / Polaris.

breaker can use for analysis. Fewer symbol instances generally translate to less valuable statistical data, less opportunity for pattern recognition, etc. The second way that one can improve the security of a given homophonic substitution cipher is to increase its number of symbols. Again, in general, the more symbols, the better the likelihood that the frequency characteristics of the underlying plaintext are hidden.

In order to develop an intuition for the relationship between the number of symbols in a given cipher and its corresponding strength, let's consider the following thought experiment. Suppose we are crafting a cipher that has a length of one hundred characters. Further suppose our plaintext message includes twenty-three of the twenty-six possible letters in the English alphabet — similar to the content of the 408 cipher. In this case, the number of unique symbols that we can use in our homophonic substitution cipher lies between twenty-three (the number of letters used) and one hundred (the message length).

If we choose twenty-three symbols, the cipher is not technically a homophonic substitution cipher but rather a simple substitution cipher that, quite likely, can be easily broken. On the other hand, if we venture to the opposite end of the spectrum and use one hundred symbols — one for each individual character in the plaintext message — the cipher becomes, literally, impossible to solve. This quality can be seen by observing that the one hundred unique cipher symbols can represent any message that is one hundred characters in length. Each ciphertext symbol occurs exactly once and, therefore, provides no meaningful information about its hidden plaintext letter. It follows that each possible position between twenty-three and one hundred symbols represents an intermediate point along this spectrum from easy to impossible.

Comparing the 340 to the 408, the Zodiac reduced the length of the cipher by sixty-eight symbol instances — a decrease of one-sixth or 16.67 percent. At the same time, he increased the symbol count from fifty-four to sixty-three. Surprisingly, the percentage increase is exactly the same, 16.67 percent. Is this symmetry a coincidence? The length is 16.67 percent shorter *and* the symbol count is 16.67 percent higher? Yet again, we have another of these areas in the minutiae of the case that we could explain as a mere coincidence, but doing so feels uncomfortable. A more natural explanation is that the mathematically minded killer was systematic in his incremental design of the 340. Regardless, the result of combining these two changes is that the 340 should be a substantially stronger cipher than the 408 — albeit still solvable — if it's a straightforward homophonic substitution cipher.

5.2.4 The "My Name Is" Cipher

Short of the killer being identified, we probably will never have a completely satisfactory solution to the "My Name Is" cipher. With eight symbols across thirteen symbol instances, it is, quite simply, just not long enough. Nevertheless, there are some interesting observations to be made about the cipher. Also, despite our inability to thoroughly validate a solution, I can offer a probable solution based on a solid understanding of homophonic substitution ciphers and a good knowledge of the Zodiac. Moreover, this solution not only makes sense from a cipher perspective, but it's bolstered by the killer's letter content and its consistency with my proposed solution for the 32 cipher in the next section.

Figure 5.7: The "My Name Is" cipher as written by the Zodiac

As noted earlier, the "My Name Is" cipher is almost certainly a six-month anniversary response to an article that appeared in the *Examiner* on October 22, 1969. Entitled "Cipher Expert Dares Zodiac to 'Tell' Name," the article documents the president of the American Cryptogram Association, Dr. D. C. B. Marsh — the same man who validated the Hardens' solution to the 408 — laying down a challenge to the Zodiac. In Marsh's own words:

> *I invite 'Zodiac' to send to the American Cryptogram*
> *Association ... a cipher code — however complicated —*
> *which will truly and honestly include his name — for*
> *study by myself and my colleagues in the association.*[8]

Dr. Marsh asked the Zodiac to provide a cipher that encrypted his true name. The killer responded, albeit later than most would have expected, with a cipher that he introduced via the phrase: "My name is."

Also of interest with this cipher are the choices the killer made for the ciphertext symbols. In particular, there are a total of eight symbols, four of which are the letters **N**, **A**, **M**, and **E**. Of course, these letters spell the word **NAME**. In my estimation, this choice of symbols was intentional and represents a bit of gamesmanship on the part of the killer. He's constructing a cipher that allegedly conceals his name; what better symbols to use than the letters that spell out the very subject of the cipher's supposed content. Would-be cipher solvers are forced to manipulate the word "name" to find a name. The killer probably found the idea mildly amusing.

5.2.4.1 Probable Solution

The first observation to make in considering a possible solution to this cipher is that one of the symbols is ⊕, also known as the Zodiac symbol. All four of the Zodiac's ciphers include the killer's symbol, which, in and of itself, is not surprising considering how extensively he uses the symbol elsewhere. However, what we should keep in mind, especially with a short cipher like this, is that the symbol is special and already has a meaning beyond being used as a cipher symbol. Specifically, the killer, of course, uses the symbol to refer to his persona, the Zodiac.

Next we turn our attention to the Taurus symbol within a circle, sometimes described as an eight within a circle: ⊗. This symbol is highly unusual. At the opposite end of the spectrum from the Zodiac symbol, this symbol is never used in any of the killer's other ciphers or communiqués. Moreover, it's repeated three times in the middle of this cipher. Because of this repetition, it's unlikely that the symbol actually represents a letter; the pattern is improbable. Furthermore, due to the extra effort that the killer invested in making the symbol unlike anything he used elsewhere in his letters, it seems to be singled out for serving a special purpose.

Based on these reasons, I submit that the Taurus symbol is dividing the cipher into distinct parts. There are three instances of this symbol and, hence, four separate parts of the cipher. In fact, there is some subtle symbolism that adds credence to this idea. The Taurus symbol is, of course, one of the signs of the zodiac. The zodiac is the conceptual division of the nighttime sky into twelve different sections. When dividing a cipher into different parts, what better symbol to use than one rooted in the concept of division? If the killer had used a more common symbol such as the ciphertext letter **A**, we probably never would have figured out the intended purpose. **A** is used in all of the other ciphers, and it, presumably, stands for a plaintext letter in each case. But by using a symbol that (a) is never used anywhere else in the killer's writing, (b) is unusually complex in construction, and (c) is rooted in a concept that involves division, we have a chance of understanding the symbol's purpose.

Continuing this line of thought, the first part of the cipher contains four symbol instances with the last symbol being the special ⊕, which probably stands for "the Zodiac." Both the second and third parts of the cipher are individual letters. The fourth part of the cipher is again a four symbol fragment.

The latter three parts suspiciously resemble a name in the form of first initial, middle initial, and last name. Here we can see that the ⊗ symbol is not only dividing the cipher into sections, it's actually functioning like a period. And again, the killer's choice of symbol reinforces this conclusion. He could have just used an unmodified Taurus symbol. In many ways, doing so would have satisfied the above-described goals: the Taurus symbol is not used elsewhere, it's reasonably complex, and it provides the division symbolism. But by encircling the Taurus symbol, the killer is making the resulting symbol physically resemble the punctuation mark whose purpose it's serving.

Returning to the first part, we note that two of the symbols, **A** and **N**, also occur in the final part. In this way, the first part may be serving as an aid to decipherment. In other words, if we can infer this fragment, it will provide us with two of the letters in the final part. Again, the Zodiac symbol likely represents the words "the Zodiac," and it's preceded by three other symbol instances. What three-letter phrase could precede "the Zodiac," especially as it relates to an identity? The most probable candidate for these symbols, in my estimation, is the phrase **i am**.

There is a curious fact involving the letter in which the "My Name Is" cipher appeared that can be interpreted as a clue supporting the solution starting with **i am**. Specifically, the text immediately after the cipher begins with the phrase "I am," from the sentence "I am mildly cereous...." Furthermore, it's positioned immediately under the beginning of the cipher. The killer could have indented the cipher. He chose not to. Instead, he kept the cipher flush left and then wrote "I am" immediately under it, as shown in Figure 5.8. I interpret this positioning as another, perhaps less abstract, instance of spatial information.

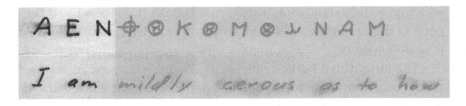

Figure 5.8: By writing "I am" immediately under the beginning of the "My Name Is" cipher, the Zodiac may have provided a clue to its decipherment

Also worthy of note, this solution for the first part of the cipher has an interesting characteristic in that both of the two ciphertext vowels, **A** and **E**, correspond to plaintext vowels, **i** and **a** respectively.

The remaining consonant **N** corresponds to the consonant **m**. This aspect of the proposed solution, in and of itself, feels as if it was done by design.

If this interpretation is correct, the killer is providing the solution for two of the four repeated symbols, and I propose that one of the other two symbols doesn't even represent a letter. It's not too much of a stretch to say that he's practically giving us the solution.

Putting these pieces together, we get **i am [the zodiac]** followed by a first initial, middle initial, and last name. The first initial can be anything — the symbol is never repeated. The middle initial matches the last letter of the last name. Similar to the first initial, the first letter of the last name can be anything. Finally, the middle two letters of the last name are known based on the **i am** part; specifically, they are **m** and **i** respectively. This partial result is shown in Figure 5.9. In the interest of clearly differentiating the remaining cipher symbols from the plaintext, I've changed the three unresolved symbols to **X**, **Y**, and **Z**.

$$i \ a \ m \oplus . X . Y . Z m \ i \ Y$$

Figure 5.9: The partial result of the "My Name Is" cipher. For simplicity, the unresolved ciphertext symbols have been replaced with **X**, **Y**, and **Z**.

Figure 5.10 shows some possible names that fit these constraints.

$$? . \ t . \ s \ m \ i \ t$$
$$? . \ d . \ s \ m \ i \ d$$

Figure 5.10: Possible solutions that fit the constraints imposed by the cipher. The **?** position remains unknown.

Both of the last names from Figure 5.10, though not common, are valid in the sense that there are people who have these names. If we take this line of speculation one step further, we can entertain the possibility that the killer may have felt uncomfortable including his entire last name in the cipher and, therefore, opted to include only most of it. In particular, if we allow for the possibility that there is one additional letter in the last name, we end up with a remarkable solution shown in Figure 5.11.

?. t. s m i t h

Figure 5.11: A remarkable solution that fits the cipher if we allow for the possibility that the killer omitted the final letter of his last name

Of course, **smith** is *the* most common surname in the United States. Certainly, the requirement that the middle initial be **t** would significantly reduce the number of people who match the possible solution. Nevertheless, we are surely talking about a sizable portion of the population.

We've now reached the point where we can benefit from some reader participation. Does anybody reading these words know of a man named [Something] T. Smith or Smit who lived in the Greater Los Angeles area during 1964 and then moved to the San Francisco Bay Area in 1967 or 1968? If you do, perhaps you can help solve one of the most perplexing cases in American criminal justice history.

My opinion is that, on its own, the merits of this solution are exceptionally strong. The derivation is logical and based on fundamentally sound principles. There's no relying on anagramming or the imperfect plaintext that plague so many other proposed solutions. But, one of the strongest reasons to believe that this solution is correct cannot be understood by considering the cipher in isolation. Rather, it relates to a synergy that this solution shares with the one that I propose in the next section.

5.2.5   The 32 Cipher

The killer's 32 cipher, shown in Figure 5.12, is unique in that it's but a piece of a larger puzzle. The missive that contained the cipher explained:

> *The map coupled with this code will tell you where the bomb is set.*

Of course, the "map" referred to the cutout section from a 1969 Phillips 66 map of California that showed the San Francisco Bay Area. As previously noted, the killer annotated a Zodiac symbol inspired by a compass rose and added that the zero line of the symbol should be set to magnetic north. These elements almost certainly represented the basis for the killer's methodology, as described in Chapter 3.

Figure 5.12: The 32 cipher from the Zodiac's Button Letter

The cipher and the map were part of the killer's Button Letter sent June 26, 1970. The *Chronicle* reported on the letter in its June 30 edition. While the killer had clearly devised some type of elaborate scheme involving the location of his supposed bus bomb, the author of the article, Paul Avery, completely missed the killer's point. Avery wrote:[9]

> *Then, apparently to seem as an afterthought, Zodiac indicated he has planted a bomb somewhere in the vicinity of Mount Diablo.*
>
> ...
>
> *The area around Mount Diablo was pinpointed as the spot where a bomb has been planted.*

People have differing opinions about the killer's true intentions in terms of following through on his threat to blow up a school bus. Putting that debate aside for the moment, the evidence clearly suggests that the killer was trying to communicate something about a particular location on the map that he provided. Exactly how the killer intended readers to interpret the clues in his writing remains open to debate. But what is clear is that the meaning wasn't something as simplistic as "Mount Diablo was pinpointed as the spot ... "[9] Given the time and effort that the Zodiac undoubtedly invested in the game that he was playing with law enforcement and the degree to which Avery simply misunderstood the meaning of the letter and the map, the situation must have been a massive source of frustration for the killer. His complex masterpiece that was worthy of respect and admiration — again, similar to Rainsford and his tiger prey as described in Section 4.1.1.2 — was being explained to the people of the Bay Area as a simplistic, ill-conceived afterthought.

In fact, it was probably this frustration that motivated the Zodiac to do the one thing that he had never done before and would never do again: unambiguously provide a clue about what he meant. In the *Mikado* Letter that was sent one month after the Button Letter, the killer provided his notorious clarifying postscript.

PS. The Mt. Diablo Code concerns
Radians + # inches along the radians

These are the pieces with which we can try to make sense of the 32 cipher. As with the "My Name Is" cipher, the 32 cipher is again so short and so lacking in repeated symbols — only three of the symbols repeat, with each being used just twice — that verifying a potential solution is an exceptionally difficult proposition. Yet, also similarly, I can make a solid attempt at a solution based on an educated understanding of the killer's ciphers and the case evidence. In so doing, we will arrive at a remarkable possibility that is supported by many aspects of the evidence.

5.2.5.1 Probable Solution

Before we get started on the solution itself, it's instructive to take a moment and consider what we're trying to find. As the killer explained, the correct solution to the 32 cipher along with the provided

Phillips 66 map of the Bay Area should enable the solver to identify the location where the killer allegedly intended to plant or had planted his bus bomb. From the detailed description of the second bomb diagram in the "My Name Is" Letter, including the drawing shown in Figure 5.13 and the explanation that the bomb would be armed in the "early morning," we know that the road in question generally runs north-south, and the westerly direction should include a hillside that's exposed to morning sunlight. This orientation is not open to interpretation; it's directly implied by the details of the diagram. Hence, a viable solution to this cipher should, somehow, lead us to a location that fits these criteria.

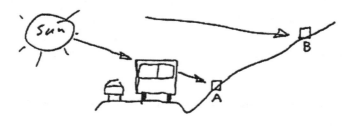

Figure 5.13: The Zodiac's drawing from the second bomb diagram accompanying the "My Name Is" Letter. From this drawing and the description of the sunlight being "early morning," we can infer that the road generally runs north-south and the hill is on the west side.

Now that we have the goal clearly in mind, the first observation to make about this cipher is that its general structure is similar to that of the "My Name Is" cipher. Whereas the latter cryptogram has three symbol instances and the Zodiac symbol at the beginning of the cipher, the 32 cipher has the Zodiac symbol followed by three symbol instances at the end. And once again, some of the three symbols — in this case exactly one — are used elsewhere in the cryptogram.

This arrangement suggests the 32 cipher is analogous to the "My Name Is" cipher in two ways: (a) the Zodiac symbol again represents the words "the Zodiac," the killer's persona, and (b) the three symbol instances at the end of the cipher conceal a small amount of inferable text that provides a clue for solving the rest of the cipher.

Considering three-letter words or phrases that could be used to conclude a cipher following the killer's signature symbol, one possibility seems more likely than all the others: the word **out**.

Military radio communication developed a protocol by which operators use a set of established words and phrases to stand for commonly used longer sentences. Much of the public is familiar with several of these words, although undoubtedly most people do not know their precise meanings. Such words include "Roger," "Wilco," and "Over." Collectively, these words are known as procedure words or prowords for short. "Out" is a well-known procedure word that stands for the sentence:

> *This is the end of my transmission to you and no answer is required or expected.*

This statement feels like an especially appropriate way for the killer to sign off at the end of his cipher.

Once again, there is a curiosity about the killer's cipher that gives additional credence to the possibility that the final three symbol instances represent the word **out**. The ciphertext symbols of these three characters are the English letters **P** and **W** and the Greek letter Δ. The killer may well have chosen the symbols **P** and **W**, which are not used anywhere else in the cipher — specifically as an abbreviation for the phrase "Procedure Word," thereby creating an additional clue for the enciphered text of this segment. Much like the vowel-consonant construction of the **i am** fragment in the "My Name Is" cipher, this choice of ciphertext symbols creates a certain by-design quality. The first two symbols are taken from the English alphabet and provide a clue to decipherment. The final symbol is taken from a different alphabet and provides a different type of clue by virtue of being the only one of the three symbols used elsewhere in the cipher.

Accepting that the Δ symbol does represent the letter **t**, this means that the second position in the cipher is also **t**. Therefore, assuming the cipher does not start with a single-letter word, i.e. **a** or **i**, we must be dealing with a word where the second letter is **t**.

In order to make more progress on this proposed solution, we need to glean information from elsewhere in the killer's communiqués. Turning our attention to the explicit clue that the killer provided in the form of his postscript to the *Mikado* Letter, shown in Figure 5.14, several observations can guide us.

Of course, as previously explained in Section 3.3.1.1, the killer called out position 6 on the Zodiac compass rose by (a) starting and stopping the circle at the bottom, and (b) centering the postscript, both horizontally and vertically, on position 6.

Beyond these points of emphasis, it's instructive to ask the question: why did the killer bother to go back and insert the # symbol in the postscript?

> *The Mt. Diablo Code concerns*
> *Radians + # inches along the radians.*

The meaning of the sentence is effectively the same with and without the #, yet the killer explicitly went back and added the symbol to stress that the cipher is describing a "[number] inches along the radians." Why? Particularly noteworthy, he did not specify "# *of* inches along," which is what one might expect based on everyday English usage.

A probable reason for the killer adding the # is that the solution to the cipher contains the phrase "# inches along" where # is a placeholder for an actual number, such as one through nine; although, the word "inches" implies the number is two or more.

So what number might we use here? Certainly, we can try **two** through **nine** in the cipher to see what fits. However, there remains one more bit of spatial information that we can extract from the postscript. In Figure 5.14, notice how the words "inches along" are centered horizontally, *exactly* in the middle of the Zodiac symbol. Moreover, they are located directly below position 6. In a very straightforward way, we can read this arrangement of the words and their placement relative to position 6 as: six inches along.

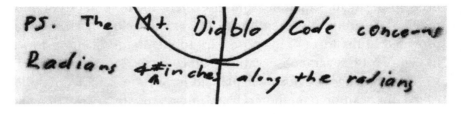

Figure 5.14: The postscript from the Button Letter is essential to understanding the 32 cipher. An important element of its construction comes from the killer going back and explicitly adding the # symbol. Furthermore, the killer created three separate instances of spatial information by: (a) starting and stopping the circle at position 6, (b) centering the entire postscript on position 6, and (c) arranging the words "inches along" to be centered directly under position 6 so it can be read as "six inches along."

The cipher itself also places constraints on possible solutions through the repeated **O** symbol at characters 6 and 14. As we will see, "six inches along" is a phrase that will nicely fit within these constraints — most other possibilities do not.

Now that we've concluded we should measure six inches along something, the next question is what? The obvious choices are the numbered lines radiating from the center of the Zodiac compass rose. There are twelve such possibilities, numbered from zero to eleven. Of course, this is where the killer's previously noted emphasis of position 6 becomes important. Clearly, the line associated with position 6 is the one he wants would-be cipher solvers to use. And conveniently, the word **six** works well.

Taking all of the information embodied by these observations and using it as a basis for experimenting with the cipher yields one, and really only one, viable solution. That solution is (spaces added for ease of reading):

start six inches along number six $\oplus$ out

I find this solution compelling for several reasons. First, the word **start** was selected primarily because it fit the constraints of the cipher. With other parts of the solution in place, we need a five-letter word that begins with the letters **st**; **start** is the only word that satisfies these requirements and also makes sense. But more than that, it's also a logical choice of words for the killer to use because it's imprecise. The man is not identifying the exact location that he's talking about; rather he's giving us a starting point. We will probably have to do something beyond just identifying the point. This characteristic feels like a perfect fit for the type of puzzle that the cipher appears to be.

Second, this solution satisfies a very important property that is not immediately obvious.

> *Every number in the solution must have a repeated symbol.*

The reason that this statement must be true is that if it's not, then the number is ambiguous. In other words, we would not be able to distinguish the correct number from a different number of the same length. To make this point clear, Table 5.2 organizes the numbers zero through eleven by their respective lengths. Only eleven has a length that would be unambiguous. But eleven inches is not a viable length because it would be off the map, regardless of the chosen direction. One could argue that position 11 could be a viable radial line. But, of course, we have several instances of spatial information telling us that position 6 is the correct radial line. Therefore, we can ignore eleven.

In the proposed solution, we have two numbers of length three, namely **six** and **six**. If a given number had no repeated symbols, then any one of the following numbers could fit, and we would have no way of knowing which one is correct: one, two, six, or ten. Only by using a repeated symbol — the symbol that corresponds to the **s** in both cases — are we able to know that the correct number is **six**.

Length	Number
3	one, two, six, ten
4	zero, four, five, nine
5	three, seven, eight
6	eleven

Table 5.2: Every number from zero to ten has the same length as at least two other numbers and therefore we should expect any such number appearing in the cipher to have one of the repeated symbols

On first consideration, one might think that since we're repeating the number **six** two times, the killer could have opted to repeat one of the symbols in both occurrences of the number. For example, perhaps he could have used the same symbol for the letter **x** both times that it appears in the solution, thereby satisfying this requirement that all numbers have a repeated symbol. The issue with this approach, however, is that it doesn't solve the original problem. If we use the same symbol for the third letter of **six** both times it appears in the cipher, that will work in a general sense. But we could also change both instances of **six** to **two**, as an example. Everything remains the same, except the shared symbol now represents **o** instead of **x**. These circumstances bring us back to where we started: the two repeated numbers can be any number of the same length. So, to make our requirement more precise, we can say:

Every number must have a repeated symbol. And if the same number occurs twice, each number's repeated symbol must come from a part of the cipher that is not the other number.

Although there are different ways of doing it, in general, mathematically identifying a point in two-dimensional space — which is what a map is — requires two numbers. Therefore, the solution to this cipher — whatever it is — is highly likely to include two numbers. Remembering that the cipher only has three repeated symbols, it's difficult to overstate the importance of this solution positioning both numbers such that they align with the remaining two repeated symbols in this manner.

In fact, if we take a step back, we can now see *why* the cipher has exactly three repeated symbols. One shared symbol is needed for the inferable text clue — the clue that yields the second letter of the cipher based on solving the ⊕ **out** fragment. Then, the remaining two symbols are required in order to make the two numbers unambiguous. Without these symbols, the cipher would have multiple viable solutions. Thus, the minimum number of repeated symbols is three, precisely the number that the killer used.

The context of the cipher also provides yet another clue that supports this solution. The killer is referencing a section of a Phillips 66 map. The solution instructs the reader to **start six inches along number six**. It's an easy stretch of the imagination to believe that the double sixes in Phillips 66 inspired the killer to use "six inches along number six," with the intention of Phillips 66 serving as a clue.

Another point worth noting about this solution is that the word **number** is completely unconstrained. In other words, it's comprised of symbols that are never repeated in the cipher. Therefore, we can select any six-letter word that has an equivalent meaning in this context. For example, the word **vector** is a more mathematical six-letter word that could reasonably fit the cipher. **radial** (as in a line extending outwardly from the center of a circle) and **radian*** also work. Ultimately, it doesn't matter which word we use so long as we're convinced that such a word exists.

The obvious next step in the analysis of this proposed solution is to find the location corresponding to "six inches along number six"

---

*Radian technically does not make sense — unless there is an implied reference — since it's a unit of angular measure. However, it's difficult to completely dismiss the possibility of the killer using the word given that the postscript specifically mentions "inches along the radians."

and see whether or not it makes any sense. Although this task seems straightforward, there is an unexpected complexity that we have to acknowledge.

Unbeknownst to much of the map reading public, many of the insets created for this type of map are slightly inaccurate. In particular, when a map shows a landmass near water, it's common for the mapmaker to slightly rotate the image such that more land and less water appears on the map, since the depiction of water is of little value to land-traveling map readers. Regrettably, this is precisely how the inset from the Phillips 66 map was constructed. As a consequence, the direction north is incorrect by approximately 5°.*

Was the Zodiac aware of the map's inaccuracy? Of course, we can't say for certain. But here's what we do know:

- Based on the accurate alignments of the Presidio Heights, Lake Herman Road, and Blue Rock Springs crime scenes, the killer used a different, accurate map for much of his activity. He may well have used the full version of the Phillips 66 map from which he took the smaller inset.

- We can also infer that he used a different map because some of the crime scenes are not even on this map, for example, Blue Rock Springs (which is just beyond the top edge), Lake Berryessa, and Lake Tahoe.

- Because the killer's postscript references "inches along the radians," he clearly expected would-be cipher solvers to perform their measurements on the provided map.

Even if the killer was aware of this inaccuracy, it's doubtful that he would have expected law enforcement to know about it. Therefore, if he had been aware of the differential in magnetic north, and he wanted law enforcement to take it into account, I would have expected him to mention it in one way or another. Since he never made

---

*These circumstances for the misalignment were first explained to me by Matt L. Miller.

any mention of the problem, it's my judgment that the killer was probably unaware of the inaccuracy when he mailed the map, or that he knew about it, but still expected anyone analyzing the problem to use an unadjusted value for magnetic north — 17° in this case.

I own a copy of the same 1969 Phillips 66 map of California that the killer used for his letter to the *Chronicle*. By taking it, applying the Zodiac's rotated compass rose centered on Mount Diablo, and then measuring six inches along the radial line associated with position 6, we find a location on the bottom edge of the map, shown in Figure 5.15.

Figure 5.15: The location on the Phillips 66 map identified by **six inches along** the position 6 radial line of the rotated compass rose. The map itself is a modern map, and the horizontal line corresponds to the bottom edge of the Phillips 66 map.

Interestingly, the identified location is a relatively undeveloped area near a man-made body of water called Stevens Creek Reservoir.[*] Of particular note, there is a single road — Stevens Canyon Road — shown near the location. Moreover, the road generally runs north-south, and like the drawing provided by the killer, sections of the road include a western hillside. A recent photograph of a stretch of

---

[*]It's hard to ignore the prevalence of man-made reservoirs in the crimes scenes of the Zodiac: Lake Herman, Lake Berryessa, and now, possibly, Stevens Creek Reservoir. It's probably a coincidence, but it is, nevertheless, a curious thread running through case evidence.

Stevens Canyon Road is shown in Figure 5.16. In terms of a location matching the characteristics of the spot described by the killer, we really couldn't have asked for much more. Also, bearing in mind that the randomness of an invalid solution could have put us anywhere: the Pacific Ocean, downtown Oakland, somewhere with no roads, somewhere with too many roads, and so on. The fact that this proposed solution identifies a location with a single road that matches the constraints provided by the killer through his writing is especially meaningful.

Figure 5.16: A recent image of an area near the location identified by the proposed solution to the 32 cipher. This photograph was taken facing south so as to provide the same orientation as the killer's drawing, shown in Figure 5.13. Specifically, the sun rises on the left side of the image and the hillside is on the right.

Is this decipherment of the Zodiac's 32 cipher correct? For the reasons I've explained, I submit that the likelihood is high. To summarize, we have a solution that

- Shares the same logical structure as the proposed solution to the "My Name Is" cipher
- Uses the ciphertext symbols **P** and **W** to provide a clue about the small section of inferable text, in other words, the logical procedure word **out**

- Satisfies the unexpected but logical property of being vague by virtue of using the word **start**

- Matches the killer's numerous instances of spatial information that emphasize position 6 and "6 inches along"

- Satisfies the not-so-obvious requirement that both numbers in the solution must include a repeated symbol and — since we have two instances of the same number — that both numbers have a repeated symbol that is shared with a part of the cipher that is not the other number

- Possesses an intriguing clue in the form of including two instances of the word **six** when the provided map came from a Phillips 66 service station

- Pinpoints a legitimate location on the map; for example, if the solution had been **ten inches along number six**, the location would have been well off the map

- Identifies a point on the map that has one and only one road in close proximity

- Identifies a road that meets the requirements implied by the killer's bomb diagram, namely, it generally runs north-south and has a hillside on the west.

This is a substantial amount of compelling evidence. Moreover, because of the common structure and the logical consistency shared by this solution and the one proposed for the "My Name Is" cipher, the two solutions are mutually supportive. In other words, the more reason we find to believe that either one of the solutions is correct, the more likely it is that both are correct.

5.2.6 Homophonic Substitution in Cryptographic Literature

If we try to identify possible sources of inspiration for the Zodiac's knowledge and use of cipher, we soon find an interesting curiosity.

Homophonic substitution is often not well covered in cryptographic literature. This statement holds true for texts that were available in the mid-1960s, and it remains true to this day.[10-12] Several treatments of classical cryptography transition directly from monoalphabetic ciphers — mostly simple substitution — to polyalphabetic ciphers, such as the Vigenère cipher. Moreover, when publications do address homophonic substitution in some reasonable amount of depth, they almost always do so by directly using numbers as cipher symbols.[13,14] This latter point is understandable, especially for older texts, given the ease with which typesetters could deal with numbers and the difficulty that arbitrary symbols introduced.

Although this is a notable and interesting observation, there seems to be little that we can conclude from it. The question of how the killer came to be aware of, interested in, and inspired to use cryptography remains unclear. However, it's possible that David Kahn's 1967 book *The Codebreakers* played a role, as discussed in Section 4.2.2.

5.3   Modern Efforts to Solve the 340 Cipher

Solving the killer's 340 cryptogram has become the holy grail of the Zodiac case. Before 2005, the cipher was not nearly as well understood as it is today. There were two key academic papers that addressed the subject but little else in terms of substantive analysis.[7,15] In his 1986 book *Zodiac*, Robert Graysmith provided the only high-profile, proposed solution. But knowledgeable people, including those at the FBI, dismissed it as invalid.[16]

In the years since 2005, many people have taken on the challenge of attempting to solve the 340 using an impressive array of analytical skills and computer resources. These efforts have not been limited to hobbyists dabbling in their spare time. Academia has published several more papers addressing the subject.[17-20] Multiple master's students have written their theses around the cipher.[21-23] In a less conventional but perhaps more impressive example, Professor

Ryan Garlick from the University of North Texas crafted an entire undergraduate computer-science course around the task of solving the 340; interestingly, the only required textbook was Graysmith's *Zodiac*. Zodiac cipher expert David Oranchak has done two presentations at the National Security Agency's biyearly Cryptologic History Symposium; the first dealt with all the Zodiac ciphers, while the second focused exclusively on the 340.[24,25] In 2017, these latter two people teamed up with other cipher experts to form a cipher team as part of the History Channel's five-episode, partially fictionalized documentary series *The Hunt for the Zodiac Killer*.[26]*,† Finally, professional and similarly qualified programmers, including yours truly, have crafted programs aimed at solving the cipher. In total, the collective effort has yielded several analytical tools,[27–30] including at least five applications that can solve the Zodiac's 408 cipher and other ciphers similar to the 340.[17,20,28] Unfortunately, just like the crimes attributed to the Zodiac, the 340 remains unsolved.

5.3.1 Anatomy of a Cipher Solver

Having more than a couple examples of what a successful cipher-solving application looks like, we can identify certain high-level components that are always present. The first such component is the idea of a key, which is simply a single proposed solution to a given cipher. Since a key requires each symbol in the cipher to be assigned precisely one of the twenty-six letters available in the English alphabet (assuming the cipher is a straightforward homophonic substitution cipher), specifying a key amounts to defining a large number of symbol assignments. The typical way in which this task is accomplished is through an ordered list of letters. Specifically, the first value

---

*I say partially fictionalized because it's clear that some of the cipher analysis shown in the series did not happen as portrayed.

†It's also interesting to point out that this television show about the Zodiac fell victim to a common pitfall of Zodiac interest when one of the cipher team members allowed himself to become convinced that he had solved the 340 cipher. Of course, he had not.

listed is the letter to be assigned to the first symbol found in the cipher; the second value corresponds to the second symbol; and so on and so forth. For example, the key that correctly solves the Zodiac's 408 cipher would be specified as the following ordered list of fifty-four letters, one for each of the cipher's fifty-four symbols:

`ilikeilingpeoebecausetssomhfntsorefnthanlwdaetorrsdvxy`

The strength of homophonic substitution comes from the sheer number of possible keys that the symbols can represent. For example, given that the Zodiac's 340 cipher has sixty-three symbols and each symbol can have one of twenty-six possible values, the total number of available keys for the cipher is 26^{63} or roughly 10^{89} — a value that is more than the currently accepted estimate for the number of atoms in the universe. Admittedly, sometimes this type of raw possibility counting can be deceptive. Even simple substitution ciphers usually involve a remarkable number of possible solutions, and yet frequency analysis allows a cipher breaker to systematically zero in on the correct one. Nevertheless, appreciating the overwhelming nature of the numbers involved can provide us with some valuable perspective.

The next concept that a cipher solver must implement is a scoring function, which is a way of associating a numerical value with a proposed solution. The goal of the scoring function is to provide higher scores for keys that are likely to be correct and lower scores for keys that are not. Furthermore, the more nearly correct a key is, the higher the score that key should receive. Of course, this behavior is ideal; often real-world scoring functions do not always achieve ideal behavior under all circumstances. The trick is to find a scoring function that performs well enough and, furthermore, can be evaluated reasonably quickly. Also worthy of note, the scoring function is a relative measure. The exact value that a proposed key receives ultimately matters little. What matters is how the value for a given key compares with the values of other keys.

The final high-level capability that a cipher solver must provide is a mechanism for generating a collection of keys for it to evaluate. With the 340 having more possible solutions than there are atoms in the universe, it's a practical impossibility to simply sequence through all the available keys. To be viable, a better approach is required. Though different solvers address this problem in different ways, almost all applications generate their sequences through some form of incrementally modifying an initial or current key.

Clearly, the notion of a key is a fundamental concept that all cipher solvers must account for in some roughly equivalent way. On the other hand, the scoring function and the task of generating candidate keys are implementation choices that allow the programmer an opportunity to employ his or her creativity. Of course, the choices the programmer makes will ultimately determine the effectiveness of the cipher solver, and, hence, they are critically important. Nevertheless, these two areas represent important variables where different cipher solvers can employ vastly different approaches.

With these three building blocks in place, we can describe the high-level approach followed by many cipher-solving applications, something known in computer-science terms as hill climbing. To start the process, the solver generates an initial key. Typically, this key is generated randomly. Once the initial key is constructed, a corresponding initial score is calculated by applying the scoring function. This initial key and its associated score are recorded as the *current-best* key and score. With this starting point established, the application begins systematically generating and evaluating candidate keys. In each case, the candidate key is scored. If the resulting score is greater than (or sometimes greater than or equal to) the *current-best* score, the application records the candidate key and score as the new *current-best*. This process continues until some type of stopping condition is identified. Typical stopping conditions include the *current-best* score reaching a certain threshold, a lack of progress, or the collection of identified candidate keys being exhausted.

The above description is a high-level overview of the process. Real-world implementations require programmers to address several low-level details that I've simply glossed over. Nevertheless, these are the key principles of operation found in many cipher-solving applications.

5.3.2   *CipherExplorer*

Having spent the better part of my professional career crafting computer programs of one sort or another, I felt especially inclined to try my hand at coding an analytical tool capable of solving the 340 cipher. The product of that endeavor is a program I named *CipherExplorer*. Like all other efforts made to date, *CipherExplorer* has been unable to extract the message hidden within the symbols of the 340. It is, however, capable of solving the 408 and numerous other ciphers that are of a cryptographic strength comparable to that of the 340; in other words, homophonic substitution ciphers comprised of sixty-three symbols across 340 symbol instances.

As mentioned in the preceding section, creating a scoring function that does its job well is an important part of creating a cipher-solving application. The scoring function that I eventually settled on consists of three primary components. The first one scans the solution and counts the number of letter sequences that are unlikely to occur in standard English. The length of the sequences that it considers is configurable. Through experimentation, I found that analyzing all sequences with a length of three, four, and five letters works well. The lower the number of improbable sequences, the higher this component of the score rates.

The second scoring component is calculated by counting the number of recognizable words in the proposed solution. Generally, the higher the number of recognizable words, the higher this component of the score will be. Again, not all lengths of words are considered, and I found the lengths that I used through experimentation. This time, looking for words with a length of three to six characters generally resulted in the best performance.

The final component that I incorporate into the scoring function is a statistic known as the Index of Coincidence or IC for short. IC is one of the most important tools available in the field of classical cryptanalysis. The statistic provides a measure of randomness in a piece of text created from a given alphabet. A value of 1.0 represents complete statistical randomness. As the usage of the letters in the alphabet deviates from complete randomness, the value of IC increases. An important quality of IC is that each language has its own characteristic value. For example, French, German, and Spanish have expected IC values of 2.02, 2.05, and 1.94, respectively. For English, the expected value is 1.73. This is valuable knowledge because if the calculated IC value for a proposed cipher solution strays too far from 1.73, we can conclude that the probability of the solution being correct is low, which is precisely how I incorporated the statistic into the scoring function.

Using these three described components, the scoring function of *CipherExplorer* analyzes a proposed solution, combines the component values in configurable proportions, and generates a final, overall score that is normalized to a range from 0 to 100. Randomly assigning letters to symbols will typically result in a score between 20 and 40. The correct solution for a run-of-the-mill cipher will usually score in the upper 90s, for example, 97.5 if not 100.

With its obligatory support for cipher keys and the above-described implementation of a scoring function in place, I completed *CipherExplorer* by creating a permutation-based algorithm that finds new keys to evaluate based on the *current-best* key. Although this part is also configurable, the approach I usually employ is something I describe as two-level symbol-assignment permutation. Essentially, I systematically take pairs of symbols and assign all possible combinations of letters to them.

Developing a computer program capable of solving ciphers requires that one be able to test it. To address this concern with *CipherExplorer*, I crafted another program — a Perl* script, to be

---

*http://zodiacrevisited.com/book/perl-org

precise — that generates homophonic substitution ciphers. That program, *gen_cipher.pl*,[†] takes as input a chunk of text to be enciphered and some characteristics about the desired cipher, such as the target length, the number of symbols, etc. The program scans the text, throwing away any character that is not a letter — for example, punctuation, spaces, numbers, and the like — until it collects enough content to achieve the requested target length. It then distributes one symbol to each of the existing plaintext letters. Finally, the remaining symbols are divided among the plaintext letters based on their respective frequencies. Optionally, *gen_cipher.pl* can add random filler symbol instances to the end of the cipher.

With *gen_cipher.pl*, I was able to create numerous test ciphers with differing cryptographic strengths. I created several ciphers with a length of 390, using fifty-four symbols and eighteen symbol instances of filler in order to approximate the complexity of the Zodiac's 408 cipher. I also created several ciphers that are 324 characters in length with sixty-three symbols and sixteen symbol instances of filler — in other words, I assumed that there should be at least one valid symbol in the final line — to approximate the apparent complexity of the 340. Using *CipherExplorer*, I have solved almost all such ciphers. The program has also solved many ciphers that are even stronger than the apparent strength of the 340. Yet all attempts at using *CipherExplorer* to solve the 340 itself have failed. A few of the results have managed to get impressively high scores from the scoring function, but none have yielded a coherent message.

5.3.3   *zkdecrypto*

I created *CipherExplorer* because I liked the idea of the intellectual challenge that it represented. I'm happy with the way it turned out. Despite its inability to solve the Zodiac's 340 cipher, it's capable of

---

[†]I later converted *gen_cipher.pl* into a web application that is now available at: *zodiacrevisited.com*

solving some very difficult homophonic substitution ciphers. Nevertheless, I do not consider it the best such cipher solver. For many years, that distinction belonged to a program called *zkdecrypto*.*

Over the years, the Internet has had several message boards where like-minded people meet to discuss and exchange ideas about the Zodiac. In 2002, the primary such message board was run by Tom Voigt on his website *zodiackiller.com*. Early that year, one of the members started an intriguing discussion in which he proposed a cipher challenge; in other words, he created a cipher and asked others to attempt to solve it. The original cipher was too short to generate anything more than a fleeting enthusiasm among the message-board participants. However, the discussion that followed soon bore the fruit of a longer-term interest. Specifically, a fellow member, Ray Nixon, handcrafted a more substantive cipher of his own construction that he also invited others to solve.[31] With fifty-five symbols (one more than the 408) and a length of 378 (twenty-one rows of eighteen columns), the cipher's complexity landed somewhere between the 408 and the 340. After some initial active exchanges, which included more than a couple clues from Ray, discussion of the cipher waned in the absence of any real progress.

As other topics vied for the attention of the various board members, thoughts of the unsolved cipher became few and far between. Similar to the unsolved ciphers of the Zodiac, the cryptogram became yet another puzzle whose solution was known only to its creator. And so the situation persisted for a year, then two, then three. Finally, during the fifth year of the cryptogram's existence, a cipher-enthusiast named Brax Sisco came forward to say he had solved the cipher. Initially, his claim wasn't taken too seriously. However, that changed quickly when Ray stepped in and confirmed that the solution was, indeed, correct. Apropos of the inherently dark subject

---

*More recently, the title probably belongs to *AZDecrypt*. Zodiac cipher expert David Oranchak maintains information about several such programs on the following wiki page: *http://zodiacrevisited.com/book/software-tools*.

matter discussed on the board, the deciphered message revealed the fantasy-laden lyrics of Rush's 1975 song "The Necromancer," with some intentional encipherment errors inspired by those found in the 408.

Perhaps more important than Brax solving the cipher was the way in which he did it. Specifically, he had constructed a general-purpose, homophonic substitution cipher solver that was targeted at ciphers similar to those created by the Zodiac. At this stage in the development process, the application was a command-line tool that read in the cipher, performed the analysis, and output the best-found solution.

Shortly thereafter, a team of experienced programmers, bonded by a common desire to solve the Zodiac's 340 cipher, joined forces with Brax to transform the basic algorithm embodied by his program into a highly versatile, interactive, GUI-based,* cipher-solving application. The result of that effort is the freely distributed Windows program known as *zkdecrypto*. You can download it† and, within minutes, try your hand at solving any of the ciphers found within its library, including, of course, the Zodiac ciphers.

From my perspective, the scoring function used by *zkdecrypto* is very concise and especially good, albeit describing it is beyond the scope of this book. Additionally, it's hard to overstate the value of *zkdecrypto*'s interactive capability. While there are many benefits that computer analysis can contribute to the task of cipher solving, there are also elements of human insight and intuition that are difficult to incorporate into a computer algorithm. By providing a framework where people can run an analysis, interpret the results, and guide further analysis, *zkdecrypto* brings together the best of both worlds and, in so doing, creates a highly effective environment for solving ciphers.

---

*GUI is an acronym for Graphical User Interface. In other words, *zkdecrypto* has windows and a user can interact with it via the mouse and keyboard.

† *http://zodiacrevisited.com/book/zkdecrypto-release*

The year 2007 was an exciting time for people interested in seeing the Zodiac's 340 cipher solved. Unlike the years prior, there were multiple cipher-solving applications, each capable of solving the Zodiac's 408 cipher. Furthermore, the programs were regularly solving ciphers equivalent to the apparent strength of the Zodiac's 340, in other words, sixty-three symbols across 340 symbol instances. If the 340 was a straightforward homophonic substitution cipher, it felt like it would just be a short matter of time until the solution was discovered.

As is so often true in the case of the Zodiac, an initial hope for resolution slowly but surely faded away, leaving only continued frustration.

5.3.4   Conclusions

So what are we to make of everyone's inability to extract a viable solution from the killer's 340 cipher, despite a collectively massive expenditure of effort? Is the cipher, as some have suggested, the ultimate red herring — enciphered gibberish whose sole purpose is to waste the time and effort of anyone who would be so foolish as to try to solve it? Or, at the other end of the spectrum, is the 340 enciphered in a manner completely analogous to the 408, and those of us who have looked for a solution simply have not been lucky enough to stumble across the correct atom-in-the-universe set of symbol assignments that reveal the hidden message?

Not surprisingly, the answer is most likely somewhere between these two extremes. Statistical evidence suggests that there is indeed a message hidden in the ciphertext of the 340. For example, when the columns of the cipher are analyzed, the symbols occur in a way that's generally random. However, when the rows are considered similarly, the distribution is more in line with enciphered text. These characteristics are perfectly consistent with the possibility that the cipher does, indeed, contain a hidden message. Moreover, people often point out the corrected symbol instance at row six, column twelve. The killer initially wrote a normal **K**. At some point later, he went back, crossed out the symbol, and replaced it with a backward **k**. If there really was no message concealed by the cipher, would he have bothered to do that? Probably not. One symbol instance would have been just as good as the next if they were all truly meaningless. The killer probably would have been happy to leave his mistakes well enough alone, just as he probably did during the error-riddled transcription of the "I've Got a Little List" libretto, as discussed in Section 4.1.3.2.

But with so many people and applications able to solve the 408 and ciphers similar to the apparent strength of the 340, it is most likely not just a straightforward homophonic substitution cipher. In all probability, the cipher is fundamentally a homophonic substitution cipher, but there are almost certainly one or more complexities that the killer used when creating the cipher that have, thus far, frustrated all who have attempted to decipher it.

What might such a complexity look like? For example, the killer may have used some number of null symbols. Nulls are empty symbols that represent nothing and should be ignored or removed. If a cryptanalyst does not account for such null symbols, he or she assigns letters to the symbols and the plaintext message is corrupted.

Does the killer's cipher use nulls? Until somebody comes forward with a verifiable solution, it's simply impossible to know. I have experimented with nulls, adding support for them to *gen_cipher.pl* and *CipherExplorer*. I've been able to solve example ciphers constructed to be similar to a null-enhanced 340. I've also analyzed the 340 accounting for the possibility of nulls. Yet, like every other known effort, the results have not yielded a viable solution.

But more important than the question of whether the killer actually used null symbols, this anti-decipherment technique represents the general type of complexity that the killer may have employed to increase the cryptographic strength of the cipher.

Finally solving the 340 cipher will probably require a combination of skill and luck. The skill will involve applying many of the techniques that have already been applied. The luck, on the other hand, will involve guessing — perhaps with the benefit of some analytical insight — the particular complexities that the killer used when crafting the cipher. If and when somebody discovers a viable solution to the 340, it will probably come about as the result of this type of exploration. Moreover, the correctness of the solution will, almost certainly, be self-evident, much like the solution to the 408 is self-evident. Until that happens, we can do little more than speculate as to why it hasn't — and, of course, keep trying to solve the cipher.

5.3.5 Epilogue

On December 5, 2020 — just before the publication of this book — a three-person team united behind the common goal of solving the Zodiac's 340 cipher finally deciphered its message, fifty-one years after it was first published in the *Chronicle* and the *Examiner*. The team responsible for this impressive accomplishment consisted of American Zodiac cipher expert David Oranchak, Australian mathematician Sam Blake, and Belgian programmer Jarl Van Eycke. More information about the 340 solution is available on this book's companion website.* The solution, with errors corrected and spaces and periods added to show intended sentence structure, reads:

```
I HOPE YOU ARE HAVING LOTS OF FUN IN
TRYING TO CATCH ME. THAT WASNT ME ON
THE TV SHOW WHICH BRINGS UP A POINT
ABOUT ME. I AM NOT AFRAID OF THE
GAS CHAMBER BECAUSE IT WILL SEND ME
TO PARADICE ALL THE SOONER BECAUSE I
NOW HAVE ENOUGH SLAVES TO WORK FOR ME
WHERE EVERYONE ELSE HAS NOTHING WHEN
THEY REACH PARADICE SO THEY ARE AFRAID
OF DEATH. I AM NOT AFRAID BECAUSE I
KNOW THAT MY NEW WILL LIFE BE AN EASY
ONE IN PARADISE. DEATH.
```

http://zodiacrevisited.com/book/340-solution

There is also an extra fragment, **LIFE IS**, that probably was intended to be combined with the final word, to form the phrase: **LIFE IS DEATH**.

Of particular note, the decipherment did unfold in a manner similar to the way I suspected it would in the previous section. Specifically, the 340 turned out to be a homophonic substitution cipher with one primary additional complexity, which is that the symbols needed to be systematically rearranged. David Oranchak, Sam Blake, and Jarl Van Eycke correctly guessed the complexity, constructed possible rearrangements through the use of additional tools, and then applied existing homophonic cipher solving technology to the resulting, modified versions of the 340. Expertise, time, patience, and a bit of luck were all required to finally unlock the mystery. Furthermore, unlike every other so-called solution to the 340 offered over the course the last half century, the correctness of this solution is self-evident, as was the case with the 408 solution.

Perhaps this discovery of the long-elusive solution to the 340 cipher is foreshadowing a resolution to the larger Zodiac mystery in the not-too-distant future. Let's hope so.

Notes

1. Simon Singh, *The Code Book: The Science of Secrecy from Ancient Egypt to Quantum Cryptography*, New York: Anchor Books, 2000, p. 17.

2. "Salinas Teacher Breaks Code on Vallejo Murders," *San Francisco Sunday Examiner & Chronicle*, August 10, 1969, A26.

3. "Code Author Not of High Intellect," *Vallejo Times-Herald*, August 10, 1969, 1.

4. "Salinas Teacher Doubtful of Names Picked from Note," *Vallejo Times-Herald*, August 13, 1969, 2.

5. "A Name in Murder Cipher," *San Francisco Chronicle*, August 12, 1969.

6. Brax Sisco (username: glurk), "The final 18 symbols are nothing but filler!" December 23, 2009, Accessed November 25, 2020, *http://zodiacrevisited.com/book/zkf-2009-12-23*.

7. King, John C. and Bahler, Dennis R., "An Algorithmic Solution of Sequential Homophonic Ciphers," *Cryptologia* 17.2, 1993, 148–165.

8. Will Stevens, "Cipher Expert Dares Zodiac to 'Tell' Name," *San Francisco Examiner*, October 22, 1969, 9.

9. Paul Avery, "Zodiac Says He Killed S.F. Officer," *San Francisco Chronicle*, June 30, 1970, 3.

10. Abraham Sinkov, *Elementary Cryptanalysis: A Mathematical Approach*, Washington D.C.: The Mathematical Association of America, 1966.

11. Frank W. Lewis, *Solving Cipher Problems: Cryptanalysis, Probabilities and Diagnostics*, Laguna Hills, California: Aegean Park Press, 1992.

12. Richard J. Spillman, *Classical and Contemporary Cryptology*, Upper Saddle River, New Jersey: Pearson Education, Inc., 2005.

13. Helen Fouché Gaines, *Cryptanalysis: A Study of Ciphers and Their Solution*, Original publication 1939, Mineola, New York: Dover Publications, Inc., 1956.

14. Fletcher Pratt, *Secret and Urgent: The Story of Codes and Ciphers*, Garden City, New York: Blue Ribbon Books, 1942.

15. King, John C. and Bahler, Dennis R., "A Framework for the Study of Homophonic Ciphers in Classical Encryption and Genetic Systems," *Cryptologia* 17.1, 1993, 45–54.

16. *Zodiac, Extortion*, Internal Correspondence (Airtel): File No. 9-49911, Federal Bureau of Investigation, Washington D.C., March 19, 1979.

17. Håvard Raddum and Marek Sýs, "The Zodiac Killer Ciphers," *Tatra Mountains Mathematical Publications* 45, 2010, 75–91.

18. Sujith Ravi and Kevin Knight, "Bayesian Inference for Zodiac and Other Homophonic Ciphers," *Proceedings of the 49th Annual Meeting of the Association for Computational Linguistics: Human Language Technologies* 1, 2011, 239–247.

19. David Oranchak, "Evolutionary Algorithm for Decryption of Monoalphabetic Homophonic Substitution Ciphers Encoded as Constraint Satisfaction Problems," *Genetic and Evolutionary Computation Conference* 1, July 12–16, 2008, Accessed November 25, 2020, *http://zodiacrevisited.com/book/gecco-2008*.

20. Dhavare, Amrapali and Low, Richard M. and Stamp, Mark, "Efficient Cryptanalysis of Homophonic Substitution Ciphers," *Cryptologia* 37.3, 2013, 250–281.

21. Thang Dao, "Analysis of the Zodiac 340 Cipher," master's thesis, 2008.

22. Pallavi Kanagalakatte Basavaraju, "Heuristic Search Cryptanalysis of the Zodiac 340 Cipher," master's thesis, 2009.

23. Jeffrey Yi, "Cryptanalysis of Homophonic Substitution-Transposition Cipher," master's thesis, 2014.

24. David Oranchak, "The Zodiac Ciphers: What Do We Know? And When Can We Stop Trying to Solve Them?" *Cryptologic History Symposium*, October 22, 2015, Accessed November 25, 2020, *http://zodiacrevisited.com/book/chs-2015*.

25. David Oranchak, "The Unsolved Zodiac 340 Cipher: Features or Phantoms?" *Cryptologic History Symposium*, October 19, 2017, Accessed November 25, 2020, *http://zodiacrevisited.com/book/chs-2017*.

26. Tracy Bacal, executive producer, *The Hunt for the Zodiac Killer*, Season 1, Episodes 1–5, The History Channel, 2017.

27. David Oranchak, *CryptoScope*, December 31, 2010, Accessed November 25, 2020, *http://zodiacrevisited.com/book/cryptoscope*.

28. Brax Sisco et al., *zkdecrypto*, July 25, 2008, Accessed November 25, 2020, *http://zodiacrevisited.com/book/zkdecrypto*.

29. Phil Pilcrow, *CryptoMake*, March 5, 2014, Accessed November 25, 2020, *http://zodiacrevisited.com/book/cryptomake*.

30. Phil Pilcrow, *CryptoCrack*, May 29, 2011, Accessed November 25, 2020, *http://zodiacrevisited.com/book/cryptocrack*.

31. Ray Nixon, "Code Challenge," February 26, 2002, Accessed November 25, 2020, *http://zodiacrevisited.com/book/zkmb-2002-02-26*.

6

The School Bus Fixation

... obsessions are always dangerous.

Mr. Satterthwaite, from Agatha Christie's *The Mysterious Mr. Quin*

The Zodiac's ongoing threat to harm children by way of attacking a school bus is one of the more bizarre elements of the entire case. In isolation, the initial threat to shoot out the tires of a bus and open fire on the children as they exit seems to have been a highly effective bit of terrorism aimed squarely at the parents of school-age children living in the Bay Area. On the other hand, the killer's subsequent threat to take out a school bus with an improvised explosive device was considerably less effective, in large part due to law enforcement's ability to suppress the threat, and later, once disclosed, minimize it.

In the end, it's difficult to know what to make of the killer's ongoing fascination with targeting a school bus. Was he serious in his intentions? Or, as many have suggested, was it all just a ploy to get attention and, in the process, waste law enforcement's finite set of resources? A detailed analysis of the threats offers some insight into these questions.

6.1   The Chronology

Before delving too far into the minutiae of the killer's different threats, it's helpful to review the exact chronology in order to frame the discussion.

October 13, 1969, Stine Letter. The killer made his initial threat against schoolchildren by way of the following few lines at the end of the Stine letter.

> *School children make nice targ-*
> *ets, I think I shall wipe out*
> *a school bus some morning. just*
> *shoot out the front tire + then*
> *pick off the kiddies as they come*
> *bouncing out.*

Public acknowledgment of the threat plunged the Bay Area into a near panic. In response, the state and local governments organized massive contingencies of law enforcement and volunteer personnel to guard school buses through ride-alongs, patrol-car escorts, and aerial observation. Predictably, the killer never followed through on his threat.

November 9, 1969, Bus Bomb Letter. Less than a month later, the killer rescinded his original threat and replaced it with a new one involving an improvised explosive device. The description of the supposed device, complete with a diagram, was introduced via the following short sentence.

> *If you cops think Im going to take*
> *on a bus the way I stated I was,*
> *you deserve to have holes in your*
> *heads.*

After explaining the theoretical operation of the device, the killer continued his commentary:

> *the system checks out from*
> *one end to the other in my*
> *tests. What you do not know*
> *is whether the death machine*
> *is at the sight or whether*
> *it is being stored in my*
> *basement for future use.*

The SFPD convinced the *Chronicle* to suppress news of the new threat against school buses.

December 20, 1969, Belli Letter. A month and a half later, the killer retreated from his previous position that the bomb was ready to go.

> *At*
> *the moment the children are*
> *safe from the bomb because*
> *it is so massive to dig in + the*
> *trigger mech requires much work*
> *to get it adjusted just right*

April 20, 1970, "My Name Is" Letter. In the killer's next letter, he tried to convince his audience that he had, indeed, deployed the improvised explosive device, but that it had failed to work as intended.

> *I have killed*
> *ten people to date. It would*
> *have been a lot more except*
> *that my bus bomb was a dud.*
> *I was swamped out by the*
> *rain we had a while back.*

Relatedly, a new and apparently improved bus bomb was depicted in the accompanying diagram. The SFPD continued to convince the *Chronicle* and any other news agencies to suppress the story.

April 28, 1970, Dragon Card. Frustrated by months of the SFPD successfully suppressing his bus-bomb threat, the killer made an ultimatum, promising more violence if the details of his bomb were not made public.

> *If you dont want me to*
> *have this blast you must*
> *do two things. 1 Tell every*
> *one about the bus bomb with*
> *all the details.*

May 1, 1970, Threat disclosed. San Francisco Police Chief Alfred Nelder decided to publicly disclose the existence of the killer's bus-bomb threat. An article in the *Chronicle* reported: "In several previous letters sent to The Chronicle since last November, Zodiac has bragged about plans to blow up a school bus with a 'death machine' bomb."[1]

June 26, 1970, Button Letter. The killer claimed he murdered a man in a parked car in lieu of blowing up a school bus because school was out for the summer. He further provided a 32-character cipher and a map, which taken together, are supposed to indicate the location where he already had or planned to set up the latest bus bomb. In closing, the killer instructed law enforcement that they had until the fall to "dig it up."

July 26, 1970, *Mikado* Letter. Exactly one month later, the killer made a final, indirect, reference to his bus bomb threat by including a cryptic postscript that ostensibly provided a hint concerning the interpretation of the map and cipher.

> *PS. The Mt. Diablo Code concerns*
> *Radians + # inches along the radians*

No one has ever definitively explained the meaning of the killer's map and cipher. And, predictably, the fall of 1970 came and went without incident. In the small number of letters that the man was yet to write, he never again mentioned a school bus.

6.2 The Bomb Diagrams

Having reviewed the overall sequence of events involving the killer's bus bomb threats, we are now in a position to carefully consider the bomb diagrams themselves. These diagrams offer clues as to the levels of experience that the killer may have had with electronics and bomb making.

6.2.1 Bomb Diagram #1

It's clear from the first bomb diagram that the killer had some basic knowledge of electronics. Moreover, as we will see, there are some subtleties in the diagram that, on first inspection, often go unnoticed. These subtleties help paint a picture of the killer in terms of his understanding of the relevant subject matter.

The diagram, shown in Figure 6.1, has three key sections, the light-based trigger mechanism, the arming timer, and the explosives. The trigger mechanism is described as a flashlight that is set up to shine across the given road into a mirror on the other side. The mirror reflects the light of the flashlight back to a photoelectric sensor. The sensor allows the circuit to behave differently depending on whether or not it detects light. As long as the circuit is armed and light is present, the bomb remains undetonated. If anything breaks the beam of light, the photoelectric switch flips, which, in theory, causes the bomb to explode.

The arming timer is a variation on a commonly used improvised munitions timing device that is built out of a standard mechanical clock. The way the killer describes it in the diagram, the minute hand has been removed. Electrical connections protrude through the face of the clock, and the hour hand has been modified with small metal tabs. When the hour hand sweeps past the position of the electrical connections, each of the metal tabs makes contact with the two protrusions, thereby completing the connection. Given the position of the electrical connections and the length of the metal tabs, we can

The Zodiac Revisited

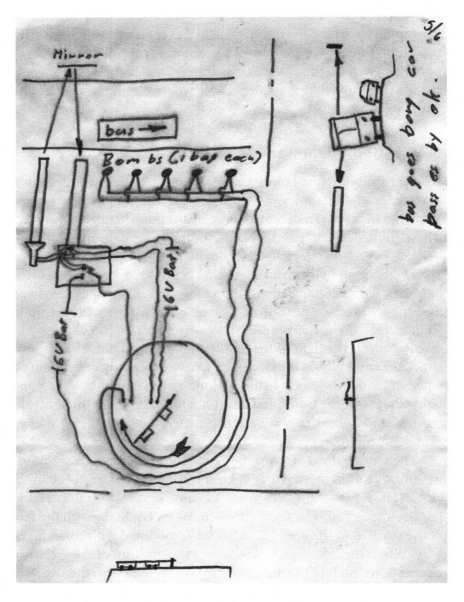

Figure 6.1: Bomb diagram #1 from page 5 of the Bus Bomb Letter

infer that the device is designed to arm at approximately 9:00 a.m. and remain armed for roughly half an hour, assuming the diagram is generally to scale.

6.2.2 Problems with Bomb Diagram #1

The problems with this diagram are numerous. First of all, it's hard to imagine that one could get such a setup to work using electronics that were available in 1969. Perhaps such a configuration could work over short distances in a controlled environment, but getting it to work across the distance of a road, in the outdoors, is highly unlikely. Even if it were possible to receive a sufficient amount of light to adequately trip the photoelectric switch, the precision required in aligning the flashlight, mirror, and photoelectric sensor would be significant.

Furthermore, the consequence of *anything* interfering with the light beam reaching the photoelectric sensor would be catastrophic in that the bomb would detonate. For example, if the wind knocked the mirror out of alignment or if an animal slightly moved the flashlight, it's not as if things would just stop working. With the design as described, if any such thing happened, the bomb would arm, and because the photoelectric sensor would not be receiving any light, the bomb would detonate. Clearly, this was not a very robust design.

Also of note, there is no distinction between a.m. and p.m. with the arming timer. Although the desired arming time is clearly approximately 9:00 a.m., a consequence of this setup is that the device would also be activated at 9:00 p.m. And, of course, a flashlight shining across a road at 9:00 p.m. is quite likely to attract attention.

The final drawback to this design is the subtle timing required by the arming component. From the figure, we can see that the connection completed by the inner tab turns on the flashlight. The connection completed by the outer tab detonates the bomb if no light is received by the photoelectric sensor. Because of the relationship between these two connections, it's absolutely essential that the inner tab makes its connection before the outer tab makes its connection.

Similarly, it's also absolutely essential that the outer tab stops making contact with its connection before the inner tab does. In other words, the flashlight must be on for the entire time that the photoelectric sensor is checking for the presence of light. If either of these timing requirements is not satisfied, the bomb would explode.

Looking closely at the diagram, we can see that the killer was aware of and accounted for these timing requirements. Specifically, the inner pair of nubs that are connected by the inner tab are depicted ever so slightly lower than the outer pair of nubs. This alignment results in the inner circuit — the flashlight — turning on slightly before the outer circuit. Relatedly, the inner tab is longer than the outer tab. This additional length ensures that the inner tab maintains its connection for a small amount of time after the outer tab has disconnected. These characteristics of the diagram are shown in Figure 6.2.

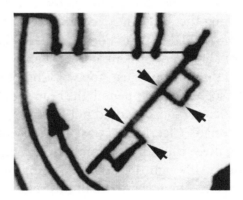

Figure 6.2: Details of the first bomb diagram show the killer understood the subtle timing requirements of his circuit. First, the added horizontal line makes it clear that the inner contacts are slightly lower than the outer contacts, ensuring the inner connection happens slightly before the outer connection. Second, the added arrows emphasize that the inner tab is longer than the outer tab, which would result in the inner contact lasting longer than the outer contact.

6.2.3   Bomb Diagram #2

In his letter of April 20, 1970, the killer improved upon his so-called "death machine" design. The ostensible purpose of the described contraption, shown in Figure 6.3, is the same — to kill or maim numerous children on board an unfortunate and unsuspecting school bus. However, the actual design is substantially different. While the viability of the described device is still very much in question, it's interesting to note that the updated design addresses many of the flaws that were apparent in the original diagram. Overall, the design is considerably simpler, which in and of itself is an improvement. Regardless of whether or not the killer ever actually intended to follow through with his threat of deploying the described devices, it's clear from the evolution between the two diagrams that he invested significant time and effort into thinking about how to improve the design.

Whereas the original diagram relied on a flashlight to provide the light necessary for the trigger to operate, the new diagram achieves its goal via sunlight. This is helpful in that there is no longer a requirement for two separate circuits — one for the flashlight and another one controlling the bomb's detonation. Instead, the new and improved setup only concerns itself with the task of detonating the explosive device.

As described in the updated diagram, the killer supposedly would have positioned two photoelectric sensors on a roadside hill. One of the sensors would be positioned high on the hill so that the shadow of the bus would not affect it. The other sensor would be positioned at a lower point where the shadow from a bus, but not a normal car, would hit the sensor. Therefore, if the high sensor detected light and the low sensor did not, the bomb would detonate.

Again, the above behavior could only happen when the device was armed. Similar to the first diagram, the arming was controlled by a clock with the minute hand removed. With this updated version of the bomb, however, there was only one circuit to worry about, and, consequently, there was only one pair of connections completed by a

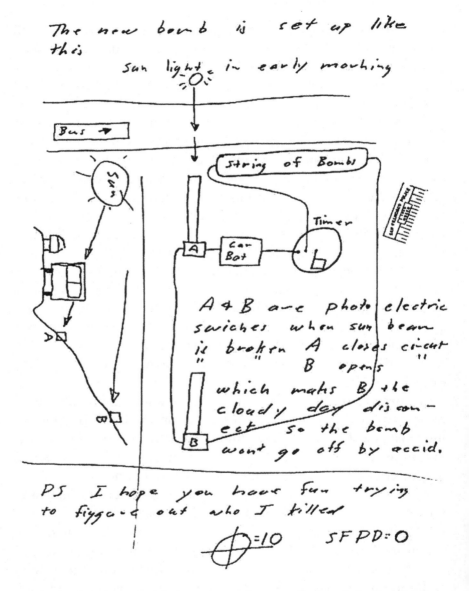

Figure 6.3: Page 2 of the "My Name Is" Letter, which included bus bomb diagram # 2

single metal tab. The connections were again located at the 9:00 a.m. position, and the size of the metal tab implied that the device would be armed for approximately one hour.

As was the case with the first circuit, this device would be armed both at 9:00 a.m. and 9:00 p.m. However, since the sun would have set by 9:00 p.m., photoelectric sensor B — the high sensor — would prevent the bomb from detonating. And given that this version did not include its own light source, it would no longer look conspicuous.

In fact, specifically because the new setup used sunlight instead of providing its own light source, many of the previous problems were ameliorated. In the earlier diagram, the task of getting the sensor to react based on a flashlight being reflected across the distance of a road seemed implausible. In this updated version, getting the same sensor to react to sunlight seems considerably more reasonable. Previously, the flashlight, mirror, and photoelectric sensor required highly precise alignment. In his second attempt, the killer still needed to align the sensor, but this scenario feels more plausible.*

6.2.4 Insight from an Unlikely Source

West Nile virus is a disease that can lead to potentially fatal encephalitis[†] or meningitis[‡] in a small percentage of the people whom it infects. First isolated in 1937, researchers made significant strides in understanding the virus and its characteristics in the 1950s. The virus is capable of infecting humans, horses, and birds, primarily through the bite of an infected mosquito.

---

*To be fair, this scenario presents challenges of its own. The process would have likely required a fair amount of trial and error, specifically during the time of day when the circuit was to be armed. Moreover, the ever-changing positioning of the sun would have caused a proper alignment to become misaligned after some amount of time. So, setting up the device and forgetting about it for months would have been unreasonable for this reason and others as well. Nevertheless, in theory, this approach was better than the first.

[†]Inflammation of the brain

[‡]Inflammation of the membranes surrounding the brain and spinal cord

The first documented case of a human infected by the West Nile virus in the United States occurred in 1999. The prevalence of the virus increased thereafter and peaked in 2003; that year, the Centers for Disease Control and Prevention (CDC) confirmed 9,862 infections and 264 deaths. Approximately 30 percent of the infections and 24 percent of the deaths occurred in a single state, Colorado.[2]

Clearly, the subject of the West Nile virus weighed heavily on the minds of the people of Colorado during this time frame. In 2004, the *Durango Herald* reported on a plan being implemented by the local Mosquito Control District.[3] Following a process that was common in the study of West Nile virus, the agency created and distributed ten mosquito traps throughout the district.

What is interesting with respect to the subject of the Zodiac, was the construction of the traps. The primary components were a thermos, a net, a flashlight bulb, and a small electric fan. The thermos was filled with dry ice and hung upside down to create a continuous stream of carbon dioxide, which is a mosquito attractant. The light further attracted the mosquitoes, and the fan was used to blow the insects into the net. The final component of the trap was the power source for the flashlight bulb and the fan: a six-volt car battery.

The similarities between this mosquito trap and the Zodiac's bus bomb diagrams, particularly the first diagram, are intriguing. Both consisted of electrical setups that were intended to operate unattended in semirural settings, and both were constructed with six-volt car batteries used to power, among other devices, flashlight bulbs. While there were numerous impracticalities associated with the killer's diagrams, especially the first one, the Mosquito Control District's construction and use of the mosquito trap illustrated that the killer's design, in some respects, was based on a fundamentally workable approach.

6.2.5 Things Left Unsaid

Sometimes in life, what a person leaves unsaid reveals as much, if not more, than what he or she says. Along these lines, there is an important observation to be made about something that the killer left out of his bomb diagrams.

Improvised explosives based on ammonium-nitrate fertilizer are a very real and deadly class of demolitions. This is precisely the type of device that Timothy McVeigh used to detonate nearly 5,000 pounds of munitions in front of the Alfred P. Murrah Federal Building in Oklahoma City on April 19, 1995. In that incident, 168 people lost their lives and 680 others were injured.

But a key point to understand with this type of device is that the fertilizer explosive is what's known as a secondary explosive. These explosives are less sensitive and, therefore, safer than their counterpart, primary explosives. To initiate a secondary explosive, one must actually create a small explosion, usually by way of a small amount of primary explosive. A blasting cap is the typical mechanism used to create this type of initiating explosion.

The Zodiac completely omitted any mention of initiating explosions from the descriptions of his supposed bombs. The diagrams showed no method by which the electrical voltage was to be transformed into an initiating explosion. Instead, the wires were simply shown going to the bombs as if the bombs would explode when electricity was applied. Furthermore, the killer's enumeration of the components required for the first bus bomb, while complete in all other respects, provided no accounting for this aspect of the device's operation.

These facts and the circumstances under which they exist suggest a couple of likely possibilities. First, as previously mentioned, it's clear that the killer had some knowledge of, and likely experience with, basic electronics. For the most part, the circuits make sense. Second, the omission of any kind of detail involving the translation of the electrical voltage into an initiating explosion required to detonate the secondary explosive belies the killer having any real practical experience with the explosives that he's describing. In all probability, the killer was fascinated by explosives and perhaps even somewhat knowledgeable in terms of having read materials on the subject. His learnings would have included various types of detonation mechanisms, to which he would have paid particular attention given his preexisting knowledge of electronics. However, regarding the explosives themselves, he was almost certainly inexperienced. He clearly fantasized about explosives, but it's doubtful that he had ever detonated a military-grade or comparable explosive.

6.2.6   Possible Sources of Inspiration

What, if anything, were the killer's sources of inspiration during his protracted efforts to convince law enforcement that he intended to explode a bomb in order to kill or maim schoolchildren? While we are unlikely to ever know the answer to this question for certain, there is one possible source that is, at least, intriguing.

In 1969, the same year that the killer sent his initial letter with a bomb diagram, the US Army — in the midst of the Vietnam War — began publishing one of its more infamous technical manuals entitled *Improvised Munitions Handbook*, sometimes referred to by its assigned reference identifier: TM 31-210.[4]

As the title suggests, this manual is full of information describing how to create a litany of deadly weapons, mostly from commonly available supplies. The book is divided into the following sections:

- Explosives and Propellants
- Mines and Grenades
- Small Arms Weapons and Ammunition
- Mortars and Rockets
- Incendiary Devices
- Fuses, Detonators & Delay Mechanisms
- Miscellaneous

While all of this material likely would have intrigued the killer, there are two particular sections that stand out based on his obsession with a bus bomb. The first of these sections is a recipe for "Fertilizer Explosive." From the recipe's introduction:

> *An explosive munition can be made from fertilizer grade ammonium nitrate and either fuel oil or a mixture of equal parts of motor oil and gasoline.*

The remainder of the recipe lists the materials required and enumerates the steps by which one creates the explosive. In the described procedure and the accompanying illustrations, the explosive is spooned into a pipe, although possible alternative containers are also suggested. The addition of a blasting cap completes the construction.

As a possible source of inspiration, the recipe is not perfect. The procedure refers to "fuel oil" while the killer calls the ingredient "stove oil," albeit we can likely chalk up this difference in terminology to regional jargon. Additionally, the recipe is very clear about using a blasting cap, but the Zodiac does not appreciate the requirement. These minor points notwithstanding, the similarities between the fertilizer explosive described in the handbook and the killer's description of his fertilizer explosive are quite compelling.

*   *   *

The next topic of interest in the *Improvised Munitions Handbook* is in the chapter "Fuses, Detonators & Delay Mechanisms," which includes a section called "Watch Delay Timer." The introduction to this section states:

> *A time delay device for use with electrical firing circuits can be made by using a watch with a plastic crystal.**
> *The procedure for constructing the timer is as follows.*

---

*The "crystal" mentioned here is the clear plastic piece that covers the face of the watch.

1. *If watch has a sweep or large second hand, remove it. If delay time of more than one hour is required, also remove the minute hand.*

2. *Drill a hole through the crystal of the watch or pierce the crystal with a heated nail. The hole must be small enough that the screw can be tightly threaded into it.*

3. *Place the screw in the hole and turn down as far as possible without making contact with the face of the watch. If screw has a pointed tip, it may be necessary to grind the tip flat.*

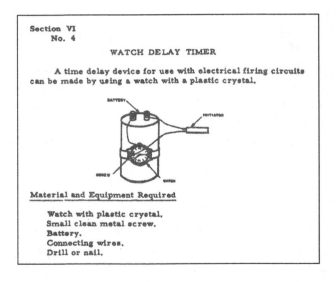

Figure 6.4: The beginning of the "Watch Delay Timer" section from the *Improvised Munitions Handbook*

Again, this watch delay timer is not exactly the same as the clock-based arming mechanism described by the killer. However, the principles of operation for the two devices are fundamentally the same. It's easy to imagine that a person with knowledge of the *Improvised Munitions Handbook* could conceive of the arming component described by the killer.

Did the Zodiac read the *Improvised Munitions Handbook* and was its content the inspiration for the improvised explosive device described in his letter of November 9, 1969? As with so many other aspects of this case, we cannot say for certain. Being so far removed from the time frame, it's difficult to even ascertain the exact timing of the manual's publication and the likelihood of somebody, possibly a civilian, acquiring a copy. Nevertheless, the *Improvised Munitions Handbook* is significant in that it makes clear that such information was available and perhaps widely distributed, albeit within restricted circles such as the military or people sharing a paramilitary type of interest.

6.2.7 Another Similarity

Yet another valuable point of comparison regarding the killer's bomb-making techniques comes from the bombing of the SFPD's Park Station on February 16, 1970, which claimed the life of Officer Brian McDonnell. The Zodiac explicitly denied responsibility for this bombing in his letter postmarked April 20 of the same year. In terms of its construction, the device used by the never-apprehended bomber was substantially different than the two described by the Zodiac. However, the basic delay mechanisms were similar, described as: "... batteries in turn connected to a clockwork mechanism."[5]

Certainly, this idea of using a clock or watch as a mechanism for creating an electrical contact after some configurable amount of time was a well-known technique used in bomb making during the Zodiac era. Of course, the common approach was to set the bomb to explode after a predefined delay, whereas the Zodiac's design was more complicated.

6.3   Conclusion

The Zodiac's ongoing obsession with convincing law enforcement that he intended to kill and injure children who were simply on their way to school is one of the most bizarre elements of a case that's overrun with bizarre elements. While it remains unclear whether or not the man ever intended to follow through on his threats in any meaningful way, we have seen that the killer almost certainly invested considerable time and effort into creating his original bomb diagram and improving upon it with his second. Furthermore, both schematics show that the killer did have a practical, although perhaps basic, knowledge of electrical circuits. On the other hand, the otherwise detailed bomb diagrams combined with a complete omission of a mechanism for generating an initiating explosion belies the killer having any real practical experience with explosives.

Notes

1. Paul Avery, "New Zodiac Threat — Bizarre Twist," *San Francisco Chronicle,* May 1, 1970, 8.

2. Patnaik, Jennifer L. and Harmon, Heath and Vogt, Richard L., "Follow-up of 2003 Human West Nile Virus Infections, Denver, Colorado," *Emerging Infectious Diseases* 12.7, July 2006, 1129–31, Accessed November 25, 2020, *http://zodiacrevisited.com/book/cdc-2006-07.*

3. Dale Rodebaugh, "New Traps Monitor Mosquitoes," *The Durango Herald,* September 12, 2004, Accessed November 25, 2020, *http://zodiacrevisited.com/book-durango-herald-mosquito-traps.*

4. *Improvised Munitions Handbook: TM 31–210,* Philadelphia, Pennsylvania: US Department of the Army, 1969.

5. "Bullets in Bomb That Killed Sgt. McDonnell," *San Francisco Examiner,* March 23, 1970, 4.

A Request to the Reader

If you are reading these words, you have quite likely just finished *The Zodiac Revisited, Volume 2.* For this, I wish to express my appreciation. This increasingly busy world inundates each of us with a never-ending supply of subjects that vie for our attention. That you chose to spend some of your valuable time reading the book that I labored over for a considerable part of my life means a great deal to me. *I thank you.*

Before letting you move on, please allow me to ask a favor. As an independent author, the primary hope I have for achieving some modest degree of success lies in convincing readers of *The Zodiac Revisited* to review the work. As someone who has just read the last word of the last page, you are an ideal candidate.

Therefore, I would like to ask that you **please take a few minutes to document your thoughts about *The Zodiac Revisited* in the form of a review.** Doing so will be helpful not only to me, but also to the thousands of people each year who develop a fascination with history's most enigmatic serial killer.

This link will forward you to the appropriate location:

http://zodiacrevisited.com/review-vol2

Thank you for your time and consideration.

—*Michael F. Cole*

Be sure to get the rest of the story with
The Zodiac Revisited Volumes 1 and 3...

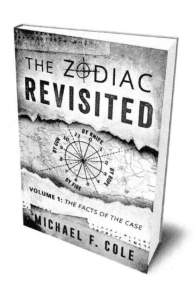 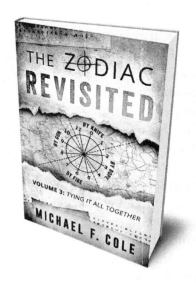

http://zodiacrevisited.com/vol1

http://zodiacrevisited.com/vol3

Index

187